UNREAL ESTATE

LESSONS FROM A RECOVERING REAL ESTATE BROKER

STEFANI SHOCK

BALBOA.
PRESS

A DIVISION OF HAY HOUSE

Balboa Press books may be ordered through booksellers or by contacting:

Balboa Press
A Division of Hay House
1663 Liberty Drive
Bloomington, IN 47403
www.balboapress.com
1 (877) 407-4847

Because of the dynamic nature of the Internet, any web addresses or links contained in this book may have changed since publication and may no longer be valid. The views expressed in this work are solely those of the author and do not necessarily reflect the views of the publisher, and the publisher hereby disclaims any responsibility for them.

The author of this book does not dispense medical advice or prescribe the use of any technique as a form of treatment for physical, emotional, or medical problems without the advice of a physician, either directly or indirectly. The intent of the author is only to offer information of a general nature to help you in your quest for emotional and spiritual well-being. In the event you use any of the information in this book for yourself, which is your constitutional right, the author and the publisher assume no responsibility for your actions.

Cover Art Credit
SHAYNA FERM

Print information available on the last page.

ISBN: 978-1-5043-6481-2 (sc)
ISBN: 978-1-5043-6491-1 (e)

Library of Congress Control Number: 2016913550

Balboa Press rev. date: 10/05/2016

When it comes time for you to write your book and you tell people you're writing a book, their eyes will double in size and then they will reflect on the many moments where they hoped to one day write a book of their own. The only thing that separates my ability to actually do it from those who don't is Marianne Shock.

I had the advantage of observing my beautiful mom write six novels all while raising four energetic children who consistently entered her office to steal focus away from her work. She managed to balance it all and inspire me at the same time. For that reason, I dedicate this book to her.

CONTENTS

un·re·al
/ˌənˈrē(ə)l/
adjective
adjective: **Unreal**

1. So strange as to appear imaginary; not seeming real. "in the half-light the tiny cottages seemed unreal"

2. Unrealistic. "unreal expectations"

   NORTH AMERICAN informal
   incredible; amazing.

Synonyms: incredible, fantastic, unbelievable, out of this world **"That roller coaster was totally Unreal"**

INTRODUCTION

So, who wrote this book? Through these pages, my history in real estate will reveal itself, but in short; I was a broker in NYC for ten years before I burned out, moved to the Bahamas to sell condos in a luxury resort and then retired from real estate. While I haven't worked *in* the industry since, I have been working alongside it for years.

What makes my experience in real estate unreal? When I questioned the boundaries of what I was capable of, unrealistic things happened, prayers were answered and magic unfolded. Now I help realtors and brokers create the same for themselves.

Though I consider my past a self-made success story, the enormous shifts that propelled me to the next level were due to the advice and guidance of others. A couple years after launching my business, I needed a shake-up. I read countless books written by power-brokers and attended seminars with top names in this industry. They told me how to arrange my business model to create a money-making machine. I would follow this advice, only to find myself, months later, in the same place I started. The game-changer for my career didn't come from the typical real estate books or the *know-it-alls* speaking to a room full of brokers. Real change came when I invited mentors and coaches into my life. They observed my work performance and offered guidance based specifically on my particular needs which was far more effective than what I was getting from books and speaking events. When I applied what I was learning, I went from struggling financially and barely paying rent for my measly Queens apartment, to making six figures and developing an impressive resume in the field. None of it was luck. It took self-discovery, tapping into my confidence and utilizing my resources...just to name a few.

There is no blanket statement or one-size-fits-all recipe for success in real estate. Brokers are like snowflakes, therefore books that preach a 'system' which advise you on how to get more listings and 'sell like a pro', are *not* speaking to your specific talents and setbacks. How is *this* book different? I pride myself on empowering others and teaching through example. This book will show you how I turned my own business around.

This book is not a how-to guidebook packed with advice you've heard a million times before. It's a journey into the mind of a broker. This involves self-esteem, the ego, how we handle stress and how our view of success helps and hinders our business. My history in this field was a roller-coaster ride and the stories associated with my deals and business decisions provide valuable lessons. However, the experiences outside of the real estate arena are powerful too. Who you are off the clock plays into how successful you are when you're on it. For instance, if you aren't confident in your personal life, how can you be confident at work? You are a whole person, not a box full of compartments and for that reason, this book addresses the journey of the broker as an authentic person, in and outside of this business.

Similar to how our lives are laid before us, the book is presented in a chronological order of events in my personal and professional life with tips and exercises corresponding with those moments. Whether you're a rookie who needs a preview of what's to come or you're a seasoned broker who thinks they've seen it all, you will get something from my story. It's a journey through vulnerable moments many brokers experience but rarely speak of. It's all fair game here. Instead of simply stating *it was hard becoming a success*, I share the details of *how* hard and humbling it was. When I say I made it from a low-level leasing agent to a broker achieving close to forty-million in sales yearly and eventually closing a deal on a yacht while sporting a two-piece, I show how it happened. It wasn't by accident. Nothing was handed to me. I had to bury my pride and take risks that seem unreal and continue to baffle me when I look back on it's creation.

Most of the names, places and events have been altered to protect those who contributed to those events, whether positive or negative.

As I use the term "broker" throughout this book, I am referring to those who represent buyers (salespeople/ agents/realtors). I acknowledge that the law of each state differs and sometimes dictates a person must be a salesperson first (as was the case in NYC). I obtained the broker title after seven years of being an agent, even though my duties and the job itself didn't change in its style or responsibility.

I hope you enjoy this book as much as I did living it...

LESSON #1

YOUR CALLING, YOUR CHOOSING

You'll never hear a child say "I want to be a real estate agent when I grow up." You won't even hear a high school student say those words. Let's face it, this is an industry full of people who had other plans. For that reason, it's chock-full of eclectic personalities. Unlike attorneys and doctors who all seem to have a similar nature, agents can be radically different in their character as well as their approach to this business and how they cater to customers.

What attracts people to this business is accessibility. The truth is, it's an easy profession to pick up, but a difficult one to master. I constantly meet people who tell me they have a real estate license...but let's be honest, unless they're actually *doing* it, they know nothing about it. Getting a license isn't hard and, while classroom learning teaches you the laws of real estate, it doesn't prepare you for what challenges the world actually presents. In addition to sales skills, you must possess enough tenacity to launch your own business. You need to learn every nook of the neighborhood you want to specialize in. You need enough acumen to handle the highs and lows of closing the deal and you need to be extroverted to the point of being borderline annoying. This profession requires you to put yourself out there and be aggressive but in a fashion that draws people to you instead of scaring them away. For all these reasons, this profession is an art form.

If you haven't started real estate school and this book terrifies you out of being an agent, good. You don't want to waste time, money and energy in a career that isn't for you and end up being one of many who have a real estate license but never close a deal. Frankly, if a book scares you away from pursuing any career, you never wanted it enough to begin with.

If you desire a profession that truly speaks to your soul instead of sucking it out of you, it's best to take your time going in search of it and not spend a dime on a hasty decision. Think of how many people are paying off student loans in order to maintain a career they don't like or those who, the moment they graduate, decide to do something completely different from their major. This is okay for some, and it's normal to be unsure of what it is you want to do. I constantly get examples through my clients who are in search of their calling and this search can happen well into your 40's and beyond in many cases. At the end of the day, if a book or a course at school scares you away from pursuing a career, you didn't want it enough to fight for it and walking away early is a blessing in disguise.

In a recent survey of office managers and brokers, 78% of respondents agreed that new agents fail at least in part because they are unprepared for the realities of working as an independent contractor.
-Survey performed by inman.com

to school, got my license, quit my waitressing gig and ventured into the world of real estate.

I come from a long line of entrepreneurs and just like them, I wanted to build my own business and *really* be my own boss. Not many professions permit this behavior but real estate not only allows this, it requires it. Was I passionate about this line of work? No. However, I definitely wanted the lifestyle that came with it. A flexible schedule was the first seductive pull and many more were to follow.

Twelve years later, I'm doing for brokers what I needed all those years ago when I struggled the most. Being a life coach with a history in this business allows me to teach the art of maintaining a successful business while having a joyful personal life at the same time.

I ask my clients what drew them to real estate? Why did they choose it? Why do they continue with it? What does it do for them? How does it enhance their life? How do their talents help those they serve? These questions lead to profound answers that expose so much more about them than their identity as a broker. Who they are as a person is so much more important to me than how many listings they have or what they closed last year. Ultimately, their happiness *outside* of the business allows them to be more successful within it.

LESSON #2

THE POWER OF SOMATICS

When I was seven I went with my family on a trip to New York City to visit my aunt. From that moment forward, my plan was to move there. Many visits later, my ambition to star on Broadway lead me to make the move and live the dream...at least some of it. At the age of 24, I arrived in a U-Haul full of IKEA furniture and roughly two-thousand dollars to my name.

A friend of mine was living in a tiny apartment in Queens and I was lucky she needed a roommate. She gave me a tour of what mattered in Manhattan; the subway system, the best thrift stores and the importance of getting the occasional pedicure.

One day we were walking to the subway. She reached into her bag and pulled out a one-hitter. She pressed the metal tube into a small stash of weed and proceeded to smoke while we were walking down 46th avenue. I blurted "Oh my God, you're smoking weed in public right now!" While exhaling a puff of smoke, she coolly responded "take my advice, you have to do this city on your own terms!"

With that one sentence, the city became so much larger and far more daunting. This advice was actually a warning that was not lost on me. Though I didn't walk around New York smoking weed at random, I did carry myself differently. That I-don't-care-what-people-think behavior is what kept me safe in a city of ridicule and judgement. If anyone tells you NYC is full of opportunity, they haven't lived there. It's a town that's ready to say "NO" more times than 'yes' and rising to the occasion required the very attitude my wise friend possessed.

I began to notice the difference in how everyone carried themselves. Imagine John Travolta in *Staying Alive*. It was a mix of confidence and ownership. I wondered what my body language would be if I was a more confident person and chin-up-shoulders-back wasn't going to be enough. I wanted swagger and a pinch of "don't fuck with me" so I moved into my hips a little and walked at a fast pace. It didn't feel natural at first, but with the introduction of the iPod and a couple of weeks of faking it, my confident walk felt real and still does to this day.

What I learned in my first couple months in NY is that I needed to boost my confidence in order to be seen or heard. I chose to fake-it-until-I-became-it and it worked for me. Don't underestimate the story your body is telling the world and, more importantly, what it's telling you.

Somatics is a practice that involves putting your body in the position you want your mind to be. It's similar to body language but instead of using your body to send a message to those around you, it's actually the process of sending a message to yourself. If you've taken a yoga class you've experienced somatics on some level. The positions in yoga promote a sense of calm and wellbeing. But what if you need to prepare yourself for a battle with the mechanic who screwed up your car? There's a pose for that. Do you want to project love and kindness while surrounded by in-laws that drive you crazy? There's a pose for that. Do you want to land a two million dollar listing? There's a pose for that.

When I first learned about somatics, I struggled to connect with it. I was in a class for coaches and I wasn't comfortable doing physical exercises like posture-walking in front of a room full of people. I thought it was silly and I was a skeptic as to its effectiveness. However, when I considered my past and the story of the "strut" I developed in NY, I realized that I was already practicing somatics without knowing it was a thing. When I embraced the many facets of the process, I incorporated it into my coaching practice and have witnessed the enormous benefits it has had on my clients.

Somatics gave me the confidence to handle moments where I felt overwhelmed or unqualified. Whether walking into an interview or going on a date, taking on a confident posture essentially beefed up my courage. Add the right suit and pair of shoes and I can pretty much own any situation presented to me.

If this sounds fake, it should. Oddly, a somatics exercise requires bodywork which pulls many people out of their comfort zone. Watch a video of a baby standing for the first time and tell me they look comfortable. That's part of evolving into what you want to become. It's not supposed to be pleasant but the good news is, practicing somatics will lead to mastering (and feeling comfort in) discomfort.

Now, it's easy for positive and confident body language to be confused with arrogance or cockiness, which I don't recommend. This is about self-esteem and an inner belief in yourself. Would you believe it's as easy as holding your chin up and throwing your shoulders back? Because that might be what you need to do in order to bring about the self-assuredness you're struggling to tap into. It's a posture that starts from the outside and works its way in. You *can* shift your internal thought pattern with your external body.

> *What's good for the body is*
> *the work of the body,*
> *and good for the soul is the work of the soul,*
> *and good for either is the work of the other.*
> *-Henry David Thoreau*

The body and the mind speak together. They do this all day. What is the message you want to send and what are the words you want to say? Do them together and observe what happens. It's supposed to feel awkward at first, so allow the challenge to take its course. With the combination of time and practice, you will notice a shift in your thoughts. Confidence will shortly follow. The more you do this, the less you have to think about it and after a while, it will become a natural part of you. Think I'm wrong? Try it...

Discipline: Stand in a solid stance. Remove all thoughts from your mind. Move around the room. Now move with a posture that speaks success. It's you at your best. You're on top of the world. You can even open your arms. Create a vision in your mind that you're surrounded by a group of people you want to do business with. Smile big. Widen your stride. Continue to walk around the room and generate some energy. Do this for no less than three minutes. When the time is up, stand completely still and focus on your thoughts. Odds are you will be in a positive state of mind. You'll be thinking "I've got this" instead of worrying "When is the next deal going to come?"

Somatics will be mentioned in future chapters due to the fact that it plays a large part of influencing one's life. I urge you to practice this discipline regularly to witness the good it will bring. It definitely created magic for me.

LESSON #3

PRACTICE AND ACTION

Practice is a discipline we commit ourselves to. Action is an event we take in order to get a swift result. Both involve change. Change in our lifestyle, change in our outcomes, change in our experiences. Our awareness of stagnant aspects in our lives is the first step before deciding to take action or adopt a new practice. In order to obtain the results we desire, action and/or practice are necessary. This is applicable to ALL aspects of our lives. If you're struggling to meet your soulmate, your odds will be greater if you *practice* online dating. If you want a promotion at work, you'll never know if it's going to happen unless you take the *action* of speaking with your boss about it.

Practice and Perseverance

Two years after moving to New York, I made a vow to attend yoga twice a week and hit the gym three days a week. I rarely occupied a treadmill or weight room before I made this decision. I set a strict rule that I could only take a day off ten times over the course of the year. This wasn't for the purpose of obtaining a 'bikini body' or impressing anyone in particular. I wanted to practice discipline to the point that my strength (both physical and mental) would be tested. I had a membership that included two locations, one near my apartment and one near my office, but neither were necessarily *easy* to get to.

In sticking with my lesson in discipline, I went to the gym on days when I was tired, days when the subway was out of service and days when there was two feet of snow on the ground. To me, the challenge was to see what I could endure for the sake of improving myself and that's exactly what I got out of it. To this day, experimenting with physical resistance and engaging my body are regular parts of my weekly routine and I owe this habit to that one year of practice and discipline. That dedication to establishing a new lifestyle reminds me that walking to the gym on a snowy day is worth it and that being tired is usually a state of mind or mental resistance. The frosting on the cake is the fact that at the age of forty, I feel secure in a bikini because my body *and* my mind are strong. Was it worth that year of practice? Hell yes!

> ## "Learning is rumor until it is in the muscle."
> ### -Indigenous Papuan Proverb

All of us have experienced practice and it's a known fact that if you want to be good at something, you must do it consistently in order for it to become second nature. For instance, I played tennis as a kid. Though I wouldn't know how to hold a racket at this moment, if I stepped onto a court and played for ten minutes, the old habits would come back. With a little time and focus, my muscle-memory would kick in and I would be able to maintain a volley. Just like getting back on the bike after five years without riding one or having sex after a dry spell, we all remember what to do if we've done it many times before. The body just *knows* and the mind is no different. The lessons we learn manage to linger deep inside until we call them back to the surface to play again.

An important key to having a successful practice is commitment. Understanding what commitment truly means is essential to maintaining your business. When my first year in real estate was done and I was at a stage where most agents drop out, I knew I had the choice to stop and try something different. I was being challenged and, let's face it, true challenge is a drag. A friend of mine, who was also a broker in my office, pointed out my commitment issues. I resented her point of view but when I took inventory of choices I was making, from waiting tables at five different restaurants within two years and dating more men than I care to mention, I couldn't avoid the facts. I was making random choices, which in one's youth is a benefit, but here I was at the age of twenty-five and on the cusp between irresponsible youth and the commitments of adulthood. Since part of being an adult is knowing when someone is making an accurate observation of you, I chose to grow up, agreed with her opinion and declared my commitment to real estate.

Discipline: Consider a *practice* that will stimulate your sense of discipline and introduce you to new people and possible clients. Open Houses are standard practice in real estate but you can expand your reach through a new practice in life. Here are some examples of strategies that are also great for networking and capturing new clients...

- Yoga classes or meditation. If you've ever looked at people who do yoga or meditate and thought they seem mentally and physically fit, what would it look like if you were this way as well? I've heard amazing excuses to not do either, like "I'm not flexible enough to do yoga." My response to this is, "yoga can help you with that." Or those who say the idea of sitting in silence for ten minutes sounds brutal. Think about that for a moment...people are afraid of silence! Silence is the antidote to an overactive brain that struggles to make a choice, amongst other things. Meditation is a practice used by some of the most influential people of our time. It's also free! No excuses to not give this a try.

- Ballroom dance lessons. I took Argentine tango lessons and started dancing regularly from that moment on. Learning anything new sets off some pretty awesome sparks in the mind, especially when you're incorporating the body. I learned a valuable lesson in focusing on what choices my partner is making and allowing myself to follow. It also helped me meet a handful of people who have used me to represent them in buying and selling homes. Swing dancing, salsa, polka, you name it, there's a neighborhood center hosting one of the many dance styles you might be curious about. Now's the time to give it a chance.

Taking Action

Think about that phrase: taking action. Imagine an action before you. It's an event that has no meaning unless it's taken. So let's take it!

> *"Do you want to know who you are? Don't ask. Act! Action will delineate and define you."*
> *-Thomas Jefferson*

When you consider what your typical day involves, you will find that it's a collection of actions. Since actions lead to outcomes, if you consistently repeat the same actions, you will continue to get the same results. This can lead to a pretty mundane existence. The truth is, we're all creatures of habit making this monotony more pervasive in our culture than not. Think about it, people go on vacation to take a break from work but also because they are craving a shake-up in their perspective. They go somewhere unique to their experience and come in contact with new tastes, sights, smells. They play like children. Then they return back to their normal life. It's only a matter of weeks before their minds get back to the treadmill they're used to. You can maintain this for only so long before your business and/or lifestyle start to atrophy and the only way to avoid that is to take action.

So, if you're like the rest of the world and aren't able to vacation more, you can give yourself a brain-jolt to snap out of auto-pilot. Want to leave the firm you're with? Take action and designate an hour researching other firms that offer a better lead generating system or a style that supports your business model. Want listings at a higher price-point? Take action by promoting yourself and networking in areas where the money is.

If you already know that these techniques will help you, why aren't you already doing them? If they clearly have benefits, why haven't you started taking this action? It's part homeostasis and part resistance; both tough to understand and equally difficult to conquer. We have so many excuses for keeping ourselves exactly where we're at. Our bodies are literally resisting change in order to maintain equilibrium. Not unlike a thermostat, something within us is always trying to keep us at the same temperature.

Homeostasis: The tendency of a system, especially the physiological system of higher animals, to maintain internal stability, owing to the coordinated response of its parts to any situation or stimulus that would tend to disturb its normal condition or function.
—Webster's Dictionary

The hardest part of reading a book is turning off the television. The hardest part of going for a jog is putting on the sneakers. The hardest part of doing anything you actually need to do in order to evolve into something better involves that tricky first step. For most people, that's a challenge. We're clinging to our habits unconsciously.

Hell, writing this book was a constant battle with my homeostasis. I enjoy writing so why do I have to clean my desk for an hour to prepare to write when ultimately I ended up typing this chapter at the kitchen table? It's like I'm distracting myself from doing what needs to be done in the name of continuing what I'm used to doing. Stepping outside of what's easy in order to challenge yourself and share your talent is annoying, but once you embrace the fact that the first twenty minutes are going to be a slog, you'll be able to power through that early stage. Eventually, the wheels start turning and you will notice a shift into a new stasis. One in which you can achieve *new* goals and even better results.

Another form of resistance to taking action is overthinking. All of us are guilty of thinking and re-thinking a desired action to death. In fact, I think most people subconsciously fall into a think-hole as an active way to avoid taking action. Overthinking can sometimes give us a pass to procrastination island (a beautiful place where nothing happens) in order to feel like we're getting stuff done because at least we're thinking about it. But we're fooling ourselves. Thinking is never as active as doing and desired change doesn't come from mere contemplation.

Discipline: Consider an *action* that will potentially alter your life. Some examples of action outside of work are:

- Take that long-distance journey to the country you always wanted to explore. Stop with the excuses... like money. I went to Paris with very little in the bank. I got there in one piece and made it out alive. You can too.

- Approach the person who's making eyes at you from across the room. If it's rejection you're afraid of, no better time than the present to learn how to deal with it.

- Shorten your to-do list. A lot of people write down a long list of things tasks and goals they rarely accomplish due to overwhelm. Your odds of finishing a short list are higher because we feel rewarded by a sense of accomplishment. I've kept my lists short for a long time and it's helped me enormously.

- Turn on an energetic song and dance around your living room. This is a somatic action that's a really good energy shifter so it's best to do when you're in a bad mood or lack inspiration.

Now that's action!

LESSON #4

WORK SMARTER INSTEAD OF HARDER

It was 2003 when I became an agent and had what was probably one of the slowest starts anyone could ask for. I didn't know New York City at all so I was lacking what is arguably the most important ingredient in being a realtor. I had no contacts or friends who had enough money to *buy* a home, let alone sell one! I had no business skills. None at all. Basically, I had the perfect recipe for failure and that's pretty much what I did for the first two years of my career.

In NYC, a person can't rent an apartment without a broker involved, and the fee for said broker is roughly the amount of two months' rent. Brokers who worked in leasing could rake in some serious money closing three apartments a week. This is how a lot of agents start out, so this was essentially the launchpad for my career. Once I got my license, I needed to find a firm that would hire me. The top ten brokerages weren't hiring agents without experience so I went to one that was up-and-coming, in a cramped office overlooking Rockefeller Center. The owner's desk was within twenty feet of mine and he would randomly shout advice at me that was somewhat helpful, but rarely closed a deal. I was and will forever be grateful for the experience, but when it was time for me to move on, I was more than ready.

The first mentor to shift my mindset was my manager at Halstead. It is still one of the leading brokerages in NY and I worked my tail off to earn the desk where I resided for six years. The first two years involved long hours keeping my head above water financially. Rent in NYC isn't cheap and I had a lifestyle that pretty much inhaled all of my cash.

While turning in paperwork on a deal one day, my manager offered me some advice...

Manager- *Stefani, I notice you work very hard.*

Me- *(with pride) I do.*

Manager- *Hard, not smart.*

Me- *(deflated) Oh.*

Manager- *Yes, you put too much time and energy into things that have a low probability of closing.*

Me- *Well, some of my clients will buy something eventually and...*

Manager- *Yes, and you should keep them in your roster but the only ones that should get all your concentrated efforts are the ones who need to rent or buy now. When you're not with them, work at your desk and cull more market information and do mailings. Find more creative*

*ways to spend your energy. Don't spend full afternoons
with people who are just browsing. You think you're being
productive, but you're not.*

The conversation went on for some time and when I
look back now, I see the impact it had on me then as well
as how his advice still influences me to this day. He taught
me that time is currency. I learned how to successfully
qualify rental clients in a shorter period of time so that I
knew if they were the real deal or not. If they were, they
needed to be able to commit to something within the next
two weeks. If they weren't, I put them further down the list
and found people who needed to move sooner.

He also told me to take advantage of free time so that
I wouldn't burn myself out. It was better for me to have a
hobby where I could meet new people and potential clients
than spend all my time at the office. I took this advice into
other areas of my life as well. I started screening my calls
more so I wouldn't waste enormous conversation time with
clients who just wanted to chat. I started streamlining all
aspects of my business and, within a matter of months,
I was making more money. I watched agents at my level
continue down the same path of wasting time with the
wrong clients while I closed more deals and enjoyed more
time for myself. From this vantage point, I started focusing
more on what was ahead of me because I wasn't distracted
by worries about why I wasn't excelling. It was this
forward motion that brought more success *to* me without
me needing to go in search of it.

Here's the thing, the story of hard work is in the
romance section of your mind. The underdog rises up
through the trenches by working long hours and investing

blood, sweat and tears. After countless sleepless nights and insurmountable stress on personal relationships, BOOM, his goal is achieved! No matter your social standing, this story is relatable. All of us work hard for what we want and we all want to see ourselves win. Promotions, money, dream-homes, you want it all and you're going to work your ass off to get it!!! But do you have to?

As a child, I had terrible grades. With the help of a doctor who ran multiple brain scans, we discovered I was having mini-seizures which were essentially blackouts triggered by boredom. I zoned out for most of fifth grade and it was decided I had to repeat it. Regardless of *why*, I experienced a significant blow to my ego. I grew out of my condition but that didn't keep me from spending the majority of my life overworking myself to compensate. I had to work hard because I didn't consider myself smart. Clearly that wasn't the case, but it was the story I wrote for myself at a young age. This fictional interpretation of my weaknesses dictated most of the actions in my adult life.

It's a little known fact that Richard Branson is dyslexic. He has referred to his 'setback' as a gift. He had to work with his obstacle his whole life in order to be a success. One could say he was an underdog who had to work really hard but he would probably disagree. He once said "Being dyslexic in school meant that I always liked to sit behind someone who wrote big." Something within him knew that his talents were probably going to be overlooked in school and would reach fruition later in life. He worked with what he had instead of trying to surpass it with unnecessary labor. This would allow him to focus on his true creative talents in order to become the industrious mogul he is today.

I'm not suggesting you don't apply some elbow grease in your pursuit of success. A level of labor is necessary in order to accomplish the success you desire. Learning how and when to say "No" is a skill in this industry and brokers don't utilize it enough. Try these on for size...

- *Stop the people-pleasing.* Brokers tend to max out their schedule with appointments with clients that won't actually close. In order to minimize your labor, focus on the money-making appointments and have the strength to say no to "clients" that are dead-ends. You know the ones. The friend who doesn't need to buy until next year but wants to see what's out there with you? Say no.

- *Prequalify!* How many times have you spent your Sundays going to open houses with a buyer who you eventually discover is incapable of even buying a home due to debt or poor credit? Having the courage to discuss finances on the phone beforehand is a skill that will keep your physical labor, time and energy where it should be spent...with clients who are able to buy and/or sell. If the buyer can't buy for a year, don't spend your Sundays with them. If they need five months to get their ducks in a row, spend one Sunday of open houses with them to cement the relationship and give them a sense of the market. No need to devote more time than that. They will contact you when they're ready. Stay in touch with them via email and the occasional phone call. If you're a broker reading this and baffled that other brokers are stuck in a cycle of wasted Sundays, you'd be surprised how many are. In my opinion, it's the definition of crazy.

- *Take action.* In moments when you feel overwhelmed and your wheels are spinning out of control, step back, take a deep breath and look at the big picture in front of you. Consider all the moving parts and create a strategy. Ask yourself "If I had all the courage in the world, what would I do right now? What bold action must I take that will create the least amount of work for me?" This is the moment when you can rely on your creativity and strategy instead of your time and energy.

But When You Do Work, Actually DO The Work!

While meeting with a rookie agent and a potential client over coffee, we discussed how his first year in the industry was going. Near the end of the session he said something that alarmed me...

Him-Yeah, I'm struggling to find new clients.

Me- Hosting an open house is a good way to find buyers. If you don't have a listing, you can offer to host one for...

Him- I don't do those.

Me- Don't do what? Open houses?

Him- *Yeah. When I have a listing, I have an assistant do them for me. I don't like working weekends.*

It took a moment to wrap my mind around this. Admittedly, there are many things brokers are advised to do to increase their business that many don't actually like to do (putting together a mailing, calling five people a day...etc.) but hosting an open house is standard practice, right? A broker who doesn't care for open houses is like a lumberjack who's not a fan of axes. I didn't say this to him because frankly, if you're new to this business and you're already dodging open houses, we need to address your career choice and I'm not going to do that over coffee.

Working smarter instead of harder means you still have to work hard. Using your mind involves streamlining your labor. That can involve having another broker share the listing but if the main component of your job involves selling a product, you should be present in order to sell it. If not, refer it to another broker who will gladly do the job while you watch Sunday afternoon football. In some areas of the country (during a seller's market) the listing might go into contract before the weekend comes or the demand for private showings is so high an open house isn't necessary. This isn't the case with most of the country so I'm speaking to the majority when I recommend being hands-on where open houses are standard practice.

In my opinion, it's an insult to tell your client you are going to sell their home and then have an assistant do it in order to take Sunday off. For five years, I never got the opportunity to have brunch with my friends. On Sunday afternoons, they drank mimosas over brunch while gabbing about their debacles the night before. Meanwhile,

I hosted open houses with a hangover. You can still enjoy life and do this job but know this, successful real estate brokers cut their teeth working on Sundays. Period.

A solid work ethic involves discipline. Discipline is the art of doing something you don't enjoy in order to achieve the results you want. Having the perfect ass might involve going to the gym. This is not going to happen from just one visit. It's going to involve a hundred (at least!). This is the practice of real estate and the practice of anything we want to do well.

Every chance I get, I ask agents and brokers why they chose to work in real estate. Most of them are ashamed to tell the truth so they'll say it's because they enjoy serving others. Once I chisel that top layer off, it always comes down to something else. Money, lifestyle, owning their own business...etc. Brokering is a service industry where the main component is the duty of moving money from one place to another within the confines of the law. At its core, it's not about pleasing others. For that reason, if you actually do enjoy pleasing others while being a broker, you truly have found your calling.

This is an awesome job if you really do care for the interests of those you assist while they sell or purchase their home. If you can leave the closing table and say "I can't believe I get paid to do this," then you've picked the right career and your clients will be happier for it. If you don't know why you're in this industry, that's okay too but dammit, show up and do the job. Maybe one day you will do something else but for now, take care of your clients and take advantage of what this industry can teach you while you're on the path towards your true calling.

Discipline

Mid-westerners, like myself, are known for their work ethic. They say, the further northeast on the map, the more intense the work ethic. Some say it's the brutal weather that forces people to work harder and a freezing cold winter definitely tests what you are willing to do to make a buck. I pray my next life I'm born in California with a destiny to do nothing but surf and play in the ocean.

I digress. Anyway, at the aggressive age of twelve I recall entering my mom's office and demanding that she take me to the mall and buy me the same off-the-shoulder pink sweatshirt that all the popular girls were wearing. She looked up from her typewriter (the woman wrote six novels on a typewriter!) and said, "I will buy you the essentials but if you want something trendy, you can get a job and buy it yourself." I couldn't argue with this, and from that moment on I wanted a job…I also spent the rest of my life questioning the importance of trendy clothing.

At that time, anyone under the age of fifteen couldn't legally have a job which put an enormous wedge between me and that sweatshirt. Aside from wanting to buy anything remotely resembling Pat Benatar's wardrobe, I actually wanted to work and make money. When I heard that the Detroit Free Press allowed kids as young as thirteen to deliver papers, I started my paper route and I haven't gone so much as a month without a job since.

A paper delivery route turned out to be the perfect job to have as a child. I got a tan while riding a bike up and down one of the most beautiful blocks in my town and tossing the Detroit News at beautiful doorsteps. However, that story changed fast once winter set in. A typical winter season in Michigan involves five degree days and I remember many mornings spent scraping ice off my mom's car in order to get to school. The weather affected my paper route tremendously. Imagine waking up at 5am on a Sunday in the middle of January, dragging one of your poor siblings out of bed to drive you to the paper depot followed by roughly two hours of driving through a snow covered street only to return home and go back to sleep out of pure exhaustion. If it sounds like torture, you have a slight idea of just how bad it was.

The gift of having a job like this as a child was the lesson it taught me later in life. Working on a weekend is terrible. Getting out of bed in the dark, in the dead of winter is worse. Collecting a modest wage for this is a small reward. It taught me enormous lessons about money, but it also gave me the lesson that crosses into all areas of life...I'm not entitled to money or the respect of anyone. I have to work to earn these things. To this day, those lessons have served me well.

Looking back, the work was hard but at the time, I was working smart. I wasn't focusing on the agonizing labor of cold and rainy days or having to work while my friends got to play. I was keeping my eye on the prize. The prize evolved from being a pink sweatshirt to a wardrobe of designer clothing that, to this day, became part of my persona. Working smart requires a vision of where all the labor leads to. Making money to buy the essentials is one thing. Taking it a step further so you can afford the extras, the things that make you feel special, that's something else. The hard work becomes smart work. The work you do, while striving for the big and the little things, becomes a part of your story. Above all else, one should strive to cultivate a beautiful story.

LESSON #5

HOW TO BE WELLTHY

The Seven Social Sins
Wealth without work
Pleasure without conscience
Knowledge without character
Commerce without morality
Science without humanity
Worship without sacrifice
Politics without principle
-Mahatma Ghandi

Money is such a seductive and tricky beast. We want it, resent those who have it, go in search of it, have it magically given to us, squander it... the list goes on. Our relationship with money exists within the emotional spectrum and ultimately, where it sits on *your* spectrum defines how much of it you own or will own in the future.

When you think of money, what happens to your body? How do you breathe? Do your emotions shift to positive or negative? When you ponder the cliché *money is the root of all evil*, do you agree? Many people aren't even aware they have a negative view of money until they work through their thought process on it. I've worked with people whose attitude ranges from sadness to extreme anger and what I have found is that these emotional responses to money are rooted in our youth.

A child growing up in a household of limited finances could perceive money as unobtainable and the pursuit, stressful. Another child living in a home with a lot of money may view it in abundant supply and easy to come by. When we perceive one person's outlook on money as a mystery but another person's view on money as obvious, who do you think *has* more? The beauty of this phenomenon is that once we identify with and accept our history with money, we can set a new path for wealth in the future.

The bottom line is: the more you practice abundance, the higher your odds of having more money in your life.

Abundance

What does it mean to live in abundance? I ask this of all my clients and a majority of them have a similar answer: to have a bigger home, more travel, a better car... etc. These things that are thought to be 'abundance' are actually just *proof* that you are living in abundance. To focus on the material outcome alone isn't enough. One must tap into the source of where it all comes from which (for a real estate agent) is the knowledge that there are countless homes out there that need to be sold, countless homeowners that need *you* to help them sell and countless buyers that need *you* to help them buy. Focusing on the source allows you to show up knowing that there is a ton of business to be had and all you have to do is take action and put yourself out there in order to receive it.

The law of attraction is a powerful thing but profit from *want* alone isn't enough. Hope isn't a strategy and to demand the universe deliver success to you and simply expect it to arrive isn't going to work. Frankly, why would you want that to be the case? Real estate is a career, not a job. A career is what we do to live out our purpose, to test ourselves, to access our skills, to reach a goal. If you want to spend your days on the couch insisting the universe send you some money, that sounds like a pretty sad existence to me, even if it did work.

Money's true value presents itself to you when you observe what it takes to obtain it. Think of the majority of lottery winners who end up in serious debt due to overspending and poor money management. At the end of the day, money doesn't come with an instruction manual but when we are conscious of the work we put in for it, we don't need instructions. *Working* for it forces us to respect it enough to take our time with it; invest it, save it, donate it and plan ahead with it.

Fulfillment

I remember coaching a successful CEO of a small business that was in the early stages of serious expansion. He told me he intended to sell his company one day but not until he received an offer of one-hundred million or more. I asked him why he chose that specific amount. This was followed by a long pause. He had never really thought about it. He plucked an arbitrary number out of thin air.

I told him "Do you know what will make that number possible? Have a plan for what you'll do with it, all the good it will do for you and others and focus on that plan more than the number."

Money is an asset, as you know, but it's also a thing. What can it do for you aside from grow in investments or sit in your bank account? How can you help others with it? What is your plan with it? How committed are you to this plan coming to fruition? What is your larger vision?

A gentleman by the name of Johan Eliasch purchased 400,000 acres of land in the Brazilian rainforest for $14,000,000 for the sole purpose of preserving it and preventing anyone from drilling for oil or clear-cutting for lumber. Think about that. He won't get a tax write-off for charity since technically, he purchased real estate. He will obtain a fulfillment one can only understand when they have a purpose and they see it through. I don't associate this man with the word greed but maybe I would had he squandered his fortune on material items like over-sized homes and yachts.

People who live in abundance and have a lot of money are sometimes portrayed as greedy. This is essentially a resentment towards those who have something others don't and it often comes from not having enough *information*. The truth is, we rarely hear about those with money who use their power for good.

Without fulfillment, one cannot experience true joy. I believe this in every cell of my body. While brokering property or while coaching, I am consistently in the presence of people who have admirable wealth and I've noticed the ones who give their time and energy to something that fulfills them are much happier than the ones who complain about the cost of jet fuel.

Let's assess the common trend in the pursuit of wealth. We need security (food, warmth, shelter) and once we have those basics, we go in search of the next best thing (home ownership, a better car). Once we obtain the next level, it's onto the third and the fourth... the cycle continues. It's human-nature to desire the next step. There's nothing inherently wrong with this, but a primary reason why many people struggle to get to the next level is because they're not really connected with what that next level is or what it represents for them personally.

Why do we have to keep upgrading? Why does a four person family have to live in an eight bedroom home? Why isn't your car good enough? Why do we need so much stuff? It's no mystery why we're such a depressed nation. We assume *things* will fulfill us and then, when we obtain them, we're depressed because we aren't as fulfilled as we thought we'd be.

The good news is, you can feel fulfillment with little or no money at all. This is a good place to be. Money will still come to you but simply *getting* it won't be the objective. The objective will become how it feeds your soul and helps those around you.

When we let go of the chase for more and consciously examine and experience the resources we already have, we discover our resources are deeper than we knew or imagined.

-Lynne Twist

A good start to feeling this fulfillment is to strip yourself bare of what you currently think success is and redefine it on a fresh new slate. Perhaps you were previously influenced by your environment, which is understandable and natural. For example, we experience wanting the same listings as the broker at the desk next to us. I have clients who speak at length regarding the success of other realtors in their offices. They describe the top producers and how much they're killing it out there in the field. They mention the methods the other realtors use. Essentially, the person speaking to me has an obsession with someone else's business because they don't possess a worthy sense of their own. At the end of the day, the more focused you are on what your competition is doing, the less you are connected with your own business model, your own purpose. Unless you are connected to your purpose, you will not experience fulfillment and *that's* where many realtors exist. They lack fulfillment, obsess on the business of others and resent those who seem fulfilled.

> *"A man is likely to mind his own business when it is worth minding. When it is not, he takes his mind off his own meaningless affairs by minding the business of others."*
> *-Eric Hoffer*

When you resent success (typically when it belongs to someone else), you don't allow success to come to you. It's a vicious circle and it's so easy to fall into in this industry. It's no surprise I notice this pattern more with brokers who have been in this business a long time. The longer they've been without their own sense of purpose, the more sensitive they are to everyone's else's success. How does this behavior help them achieve their own goals? It doesn't.

If you are struggling with the success of others, I encourage you to alter your view of their behavior from resenting it to copying it. For example, I was working with a seasoned realtor who has been planning his exit strategy from real estate to retirement. He pointed out a rookie agent who joined his office and was showing enormous success for someone so new. My client told me about how the new agent already has listings and he's photographing them with drones...

"DRONES - what's happening to this business? I don't recognize it anymore. I don't get the social media marketing and what is a snap-chat?"

Clearly he's not frustrated with the industry; he's frustrated that he can't keep up with it. It's getting away from him because the new business model is nothing like how it was when he started and he's tired of playing catch-up. His complaints hit a fever-pitch with him threatening to call the FAA on this agent because the drones might be a flight risk. I advised him to pause, close his eyes, take some deep breaths and silence the chatter in his mind. Then I said...

"I have a question, calling the FAA, how will this help your business?"

This was followed with silence. He couldn't argue with that. We brainstormed his options from a different vantage point. By the end of the meeting, he decided to hire the rookie to take drone photos of his own listings!

We don't always have to look to the giants for examples of how to be a success. Sometimes it's the annoying agent two desks away from yours who has great ideas that could potentially change your business. Ultimately, your odds of success are greater if you remain focused on your own business and simply view the success of others as an example of what's possible rather than a competition.

For those who are lacking a sense of fulfillment while evaluating their business and purpose, I urge them to take a break from work. I'm not suggesting a vacation. This isn't about escaping into distraction. It's more a call-to-action which requires stepping away from your desk and connecting with who you were when you started out and what you wanted for yourself. Going for a hike through nature might inspire the thoughts that are struggling to present themselves in the office environment. Many times people panic and push themselves harder when what they need to do is the opposite and quiet the thought-engine that's spinning out of control. Pushing yourself away from the computer, turning off the phone and connecting with your intention and purpose will help to silence the mental chatter and return you to your vision of the successful future you originally saw for yourself. This must be a practice you indoctrinate for the long-run - once a day or once a week, even. Consistent practice is necessary because odds are slim you'll make a big discovery on the first attempt. It will eventually be a natural habit that's just a part of you.

Consider the fact that many companies take week-long team retreats in order to motivate their office to achieve higher numbers. We don't have that luxury in the world of self-employment and for that reason, people in this industry need to do this for themselves. Without upper management pushing you to succeed, you must rely on yourself to create the same effect. This is why coaches and mentors are such a powerful force in this industry. I have utilized coaches and all of them have been a guiding force and game-changer. They help me see the forest for the trees so I can create larger goals with a wider view of what's available to me.

Manifesting

Setting goals is necessary to get you a step closer to your dream, but goals are not nearly as powerful as manifesting. Let's face it, having a clear vision of a future that excites you is what gets you out of bed in the morning, not goals.

Some criticize the validity of manifestation but frankly, the proof that manifestation works already exists in your own life. You are living the life you have been subconsciously manifesting from youth onwards. Where you are at this moment wasn't an accident. The college you went to, the person you married, the home you own, all of these events were determined within the scope of your standards every step of the way. Therefore, if your standards are low, the ability to upgrade will be a struggle for sure. If the outcome you desire seems impossible, raising your standards is a large part of the process.

For instance, you're overworked and want fewer listings. In order to maintain the same income or make more money, you will need to sell homes at a higher price-point. The thing is, you're surrounded by low price-point sellers... your standards are set in this place. The first step in moving towards your desired outcome is to see yourself five years from now selling homes at a substantially higher price-point.

Now, work your way backwards from that outcome. Picture yourself four years from now, three years from now, and so on. Continue until you reach where you are in this moment. This requires paying attention to the details inside the vision and taking note of what choices are being made in order to get you to that next level. This won't work unless you believe that the end result is absolutely possible and the only thing that needs to be addressed is identifying the steps you visualized that got you there. Now, what is the first step you need to take today based on that timeline?

You've unconsciously been doing this your whole life. As I mentioned earlier, you are where you are because your standards brought you to this place. Something within you decided that this is where you would end up. If you want to experience an enormous shift in your outcomes, start with your standards. Raise your standards (meaning decline engaging in opportunities below your standards) and place yourself in a setting where your new standards are maintained. I would do this in small steps since it's almost impossible to sell luxury real estate the day after you get your license (though some realtors do). Steps are necessary. It's like a dial in your mind. When you want to, and you are ready, turn the dial up a notch. This is an absolutely necessary process, especially if you need to move out of a plateau in your business.

Discipline: Turn off all distractions. This includes the sound of your phone, television, computer, music, etc. Sit in silence. Close your eyes and prepare to flex your imagination muscle. Envision yourself ten years from now. What does your life look like? What does your house look like? What kind of car do you drive? Where are you located?

To what philanthropic cause do you donate your time and/ or money? Do you have a second home somewhere? If you haven't considered that, do it now. Imagine you have three homes. Where are they? If you want children, how many do you have? If you go on adventures, where do you go? If you aren't in a relationship, do you want one? You don't have to picture what they look like necessarily. Just know that this person is there. Sit with these thoughts. Allow them to sink into your subconscious, the place where your standards live. Stay with this image long enough to feel that this is real. Don't judge, criticize, over-analyze or debate the meaning of what is coming to you. The more at ease you are with this image of the future, the higher the odds are that it will happen. This practice involves raising your subconscious standard of living. When you talk about the future with the people in your life, this is what you describe to them. When I talk about my future, I tell people *I will have a home in Costa Rica and will spend seven or more months of the year there. It will double as a retreat center for those who need an escape, meditation and coaching. I will travel the world to various business retreats and also speak to large groups of people regarding the work I do. I will have a couple horses and some dogs and will feel satisfied and fulfilled by my personal and professional life.*

Notice how I am saying, "I **will** have..." instead of "it would be nice to have..." You WILL have or you WON'T have. That's what manifestation is. Change what is already being manifested with your limited standards into what seems unrealistic or amazing and then focus on the work you must do to achieve this. The more you manifest this, the more natural and possible it will become.

LESSON #6

IN A CRISIS? ASK FOR HELP

After the economic crash in 2008, brokers were dropping like flies. My own situation was pretty bleak as well. I was living in a ground-floor apartment the size of my current bedroom with a sensitive fuse box and the occasional visit from a mouse...or it could have been a rat...I really don't want to think about it. Anyway, I cried myself to sleep every night not for weeks, but for months on end. It didn't help that I was in an intense relationship nearing its own demise. I felt like I was completely in the dark as to what I was supposed to do and it didn't help that there wasn't a single deal in the pipeline for me professionally.

Rock-bottom hit when I started paying the rent with credit cards. I spent weeks brainstorming my options with the most obvious one being a move out of New York, but the idea was too painful to bare. Was I really going to leave this city with nothing to show for the time I put into it? I always knew I wasn't going to stay in NYC long-term but I wasn't ready to leave just yet. I needed to create a strategy so I could have an exit I would be proud of. I decided I'd move away in three years and make a ton of money until that day came. Then, to make this vision a reality, I took action. I asked for help.

I emailed my old friend and broker who once occupied a desk next to mine. After only one month in the industry, he took me to lunch in exchange for some advice. He was debating whether he should leave the firm and partner up with a friend who had high-priced listings at another brokerage. I advised him to pack up his desk and he did so the following day. Partnering with his friend catapulted his career, just as I knew it would.

When I reached out to him, I told him my business had hit a wall and I was curious if he knew of any brokers who were in need of an assistant. This was hard for me. I had been working independently for three years and frankly, I had never been an assistant to anyone my whole life. To make this humbling shift at this stage of my career would be a huge step backwards. He responded with, *"I was offered an interview to sell a luxury condo development. I can't take it. Maybe you could interview for it?"*

Now, a job like this can make six figures and is typically given to brokers who have a history in development sales which I had never done, but I was desperate so I said, "YES, I WANT THAT INTERVIEW!" I had three days to collect my thoughts and prepare. I was told to bring a resume but with my history in the business, I chose not to. I had nothing to put on paper.

The morning of the interview I was completely flustered. I was too desperate for the job to think straight. I put on my best suit, took a look in the mirror and thought, *you're screwed. You're a fraud. You don't deserve this job. They're not going to hire you.* At this moment something shifted in me. Enormous fear took over. I knew that if I kept that thought, I shouldn't bother going to the interview because I would completely humiliate myself. See the power of the mind at play here? In a panic, I had no choice but to change the script. *You are the only one for this job, regardless of your experience. What's going to get you the job is something beyond what the others have. You have to reach deep and find something strong within you and dammit you need to do it now!* And then I remembered a somatic technique I learned from a coach. I told you I'd mention somatics a lot in this book.

Facing my mirror, I took my hands and held them open like I was in preparation for a hug. I clapped them together. The sound echoed like thunder through my tiny apartment. I closed my eyes and vigorously rubbed my hands together to create friction, then held them ten inches apart. I felt a ball of energy in my hands. I took a deep inhale and envisioned myself as an unstoppable force of nature. I opened my eyes and saw someone else looking back at me. I saw a warrior who couldn't be stopped. That energy stayed with me as I grabbed my bag and walked out the door.

I could go into the specifics of that interview on that sunny day on a high floor overlooking Central Park with five men of enormous power, but the details evade me. The only thing I remember is one of them telling me *"You have never sold in a development or even represented a buyer for a development? You haven't even done a rental in a development? You have no experience for this."*

Without even a second to stop myself I said, "You're right. I don't. Which means I'm going to work 100% harder than the agents in your waiting room." I said this with such conviction that once the words left me, I knew the job was mine. That year I sold sixty condos along with my team and sold an additional handful of homes close to a million dollars each. My income tripled and it was the first time I made six figures. Once the development was done, I immediately took an offer for another building with sixty more condos to sell.

The power of the mind is not a foreign concept, but rarely do people consider the power of the body. My warrior clap that day changed my vision of myself, changed my posture, changed my life. One simple action snapped me out of whatever script was trying to hold me back and forced me to tap into a confidence I never knew I had. A confidence that has maintained itself all these years later.

Successful people all share a similar talent; they have a heightened sense of opportunities as well as resources and they aren't afraid to put them to actual use. Every success story, yours included, originates from an opportunity. Being able to identify with an opportunity is the key ingredient. Once you connect with it, follow through in your pursuit by tapping into and utilizing your resources.

Examples of opportunities are...

- Take advice. You might be too proud to take it, but listen anyway. If you don't agree, discard it but give it a chance by hearing it out.

- Go to any and every event you are invited to. Practice your "I'm a real estate broker..." introduction so you sound intelligent in your field and confident in the service you provide. Many brokers sound shy when they talk about what they do. Don't be that broker.

- Help others. Some call this paying it forward, I call it kindness. This comes back to you ten-fold.

Examples of Resources are...

- Hire an assistant. If you don't have the time to do things that need attention, you need help. If you're hosting an event, hire someone to assist you. If your home or desk needs organizing, hire someone to help you. If you need clarity on how you are running your business, hire a coach to co-create a solution.

- Use your connections. Reach out to people you know if you need help. Can't host two open houses at once? Arrange for another broker to help. Have a lot of listings and not enough free time? Partner with another broker to share each other's listings and labor. Create a team in order to manage all the expectations of the client.

- Power Teams. Create a leads group or build a group of people that aren't real estate brokers. They will create a funnel of business within the family. One mortgage broker, one attorney, one accountant, etc. When they need to buy or sell, you're their go-to broker.

Most importantly, ask for help! You'd be amazed what you can obtain from ditching the pride and the ego; both character flaws that are consumed with how we look to others and keep us from getting to the next level. Ask your clients to refer you to their friends. Ask your manager to sit down and have a strategy session. Ask your guardian angels to give you the strength you need before your next listing appointment. Ask!

LESSON #7

WHO ARE YOU?

Big question, right? Ask someone this question and it elicits a full range of answers from how tall they are to how many kids they have. Frankly, this is a question that can be answered with one word: Me.

Your character is linked to the soul. It's something you have the moment you're born. If you had a twin, you would still have a unique difference that sets you apart. So, being that you are uniquely different, what is it that makes you this way? What is your character?

Why does this matter in real estate? Simple answer to that: it's what sets you apart from other brokers. Therefore, the more you understand it, the more you can use it to your advantage.

How do people perceive you? What mood do you carry when you enter a room? How do you "show up" in the world? These are the questions I ask all my clients, whether they work in real estate or not.

Charisma

Think of THAT person. You know the one. The man or woman whom you are drawn to based on energy and sheer magnetism. The kind of person that gets what they want with just a few choice words. It's as if hope and promise ooze out of their pores. Many ponder whether charisma is a quality one is gifted with at birth. Is it? I'll be honest, I don't have the answer for that, but there's no harm in trying to have it now. Start with asking what charisma is to you.

When you complete a conversation with someone who has charisma, what do you remember the most? Maybe they were entertaining with enormous character or maybe they maintained eye contact and seemed totally focused on what you were saying. Truthfully, the loud and entertaining type might have terrible listening skills and the person who appears to be hanging on your every word might actually be thinking about whether his dry-cleaning is ready for pick up. Have you ever heard the saying *he has nothing but ones rolled up inside him*? Maybe I made that up. I don't remember. It basically means that there's a one-hundred dollar bill wrapped around something of little value. The value is only on the surface and it's making you think it's on the inside too, but it isn't. This kind of person lacks integrity. Don't be this person. Ultimately, one's charisma has little to no value if it doesn't serve others in some way. This means you can have something better than charisma if you focus more on being kind and generous instead of funny or interesting. Those who understand this do very well in real estate.

Once you master the ability to really listen to your clients, add some energy to it and BAM! Charisma. This is the recipe that will inspire the part of you that you haven't met yet. This higher self truly cares for the person who is speaking and offers suggestions based on their needs, not your opinion of the subject. How often have you considered the effect your words and presence have on people? The ability to listen without projecting your agenda or opinion onto people is powerful. Start practicing this with your friends and family to gain some skill. It's not easy. It's natural to feel like your opinion is important and should be heard. Resist this urge. Make the conversation more about the other person and not about you and see what happens.

You can have all the "charisma" in the world, but if you can't back it up with integrity and results, charisma is just smoke and mirrors.

Many clients ask me to help them with their confidence. There are many discoveries made through the course of our coach sessions that will help them tap into it but learning this overnight isn't possible. Due to my history in theatre, confidence was never an issue for me. I could stand in front of three hundred people and make them laugh or cry. This definitely boosted my confidence. But how can the everyday Joe tap into that? I'd have to write a whole separate book for that subject alone. I'll tell you this, if you live a life of truth and integrity, you'll never have to prove anything to anyone. That to me is the essence of confidence. When you truly believe in yourself and you lead an honest life, your confidence will be substantially higher than those who don't. Fake-it-to-make-it works, but the point is to eventually turn the fake into something real. Try it and see what happens. You might be shocked that after a while, it becomes natural to you. It will take practice but as I mentioned many times over, practice is the only thing that will lead to mastery.

Body Language

I'm five feet three inches tall and, while working alongside high ranking men in the industry, my body language said "take me seriously." I wore heels a lot and usually stood with my hands on my hips or crossed in front of me. This gave me height and a strong, stable presence. My face was sullen and during meetings with developers or people of authority, I covered my mouth with my hand in order to intensify the eye-contact. This is somatics at play. I was creating a physical identity and it worked for me. This position wasn't about charisma and though it helped me make money, it made me unapproachable and, at times, standoffish. I wanted to be taken seriously, but I was overcompensating. It unfortunately became a part of me. I was being financially rewarded for this body language but it was limiting my experience in other areas. I didn't understand this until I learned somatic exercises.

There's an exercise that involves practicing openness and when I learned this, it was unbearable for me at first. This posture involves standing with arms open (like you're about to hug someone), head tilted lightly to the side and a smile on your face. Just typing that was hard for me. Why? Because we train ourselves how to *be*. I trained myself to stand with authority for years and that's the complete opposite from openness. After a while, I had convinced myself and everyone around me that I was a professional to be taken very seriously, but it made me guarded and unapproachable. Now think of someone with confidence who gets what they want based on their openness and kindness. I can guarantee they aren't crossing their arms nor do they have a stern face.

The power of the mind and the body working together is not to be underestimated. Ever pass a reflective surface and feel the shock when you don't recognize yourself? Your posture is slumped, there's a hurried quality to your gait, you aren't the lively physical self you used to be? It's not age, lack of gym-time or missed yoga classes. Your body pays the price for life experience. Once I became aware of how I carried myself, I made changes and now I'm far more open than I use to be and I'm noticing huge shifts. I'm approachable and I attract people I want to come into my space. This is not the case with most people. Many clients come to me with a posture that screams "stand back" and, in the world of sales, this isn't a money-maker.

During a recent coaching session with a broker, I asked her to describe a typical day on the job. Her hands were clenched into fists while she discussed her marketing strategy and her lack of clients. Her body was a metaphor for what was happening to her professionally: tension, constraint, repression, tightness. I reached over and opened her hands while she discussed the decline of her business. Water cannot flow into a glass turned upside down and abundance cannot enter a closed body or mind. After weeks of working with her on a somatic level and opening her body to possibilities and energy, her business started to shift in a more positive and productive direction. Months after we finished our sessions, I heard through the grapevine that her listings doubled and that she's a more positive person than she was before. Of course I was overjoyed with this news but more importantly, her needs were addressed and now she can reap the rewards of having opened herself up. And that's so much more powerful than just finances.

The Myth of the Power Broker

Every agency has one. The broker in the spotlight who has countless high-end listings and a team to sell them. Under this titan are the top brokers of the offices and the managers who present their success as a way to inspire the tribe during sales meetings. Award ceremonies are an opportunity to honor those who procured the most business/money. This is primitive behavior at its best. Whoever is hunting and gathering the most must be acknowledged in order to maintain their momentum or they will feel unappreciated, their productivity will lessen and the tribe will starve. They are also an example of what to strive for. But in modern-day psychology, the outcome of these parades and hierarchy isn't always inspiration. It can be anything from resentment to shame.

It's a benefit to your business to have an ideal to strive for, but when the high-grossing outcome doesn't materialize, disappointment sets in and that's when the limiting beliefs start.

When brokers compare their success against the high ranking, they're engaging in a shame spiral. It's an internal conversation they have with themselves. Like a parrot on their shoulder constantly reminding them where they are in comparison to where they're supposed to be. Of course this doesn't apply to just real estate. This happens in our social lives, with our friends, with our family. The parrot squawks...

"You don't have a date to the wedding. People are going to feel sorry for you"

"Why would she go on a date with you when she has so many attractive guys to choose from?"

"The top broker did thirty-four million in sales last year. What did you sell?"

This is the ego talking. We think of the ego as the inflated self, telling us how awesome and amazing we are. For example, when you're around someone who is bragging about his car or how many deals he closed last week, you might say "he's egotistical" and you'd be right. This man's self-worth and ego are relying on each other. But the ego is more complicated than this. It's the voice within constantly telling you when you're great *and* when you aren't. Essentially, both outlooks involve a platform in which you are comparing yourself to something or someone else. Your ego tells you how you measure up. The pendulum swings to the left and to the right where "I'm amazing" is on one side and "I stink" is on the other.

So how do we release ourselves from this burden so we can actually focus on our work and be our highest self? How do we stop the pendulum from swinging and center it so that we don't suffer at the hands of that emotionally charged, ego voice within? Easy, observe the voice. That's the first step and it may be the only one you need. Instead of just going about your day and ignoring the voice or fighting the voice, be aware of it. Take note of what it's saying and why. Once you identify with this inner voice, with the ego, you will come face to face with what is limiting your performance.

The steps that follow this observational skill involve a trip into the past and what the ego has to say about it. For example, imagine someone who considers himself an underdog working tirelessly to prove what he's capable of but, despite this, he never quite reaches his destination because the ego IS the underdog within. The ego protects itself and essentially says *"No, this is working just fine. We're great the way we are. Continue to work your tail off."* In order for this person to experience fulfillment, he needs to confront his ego and witness the story that's been driving him his whole life. Once we see the power of this story, we are able to rewrite it. That's correct, you can rewrite history. Once this happens, you have the clean slate to redefine your OWN idea of what success is; not the one that's been running the show alongside your ego all this time. Soon the comparisons will diminish and the focus will be on your own work and less on what others are doing.

Exercise: Close your eyes and imagine before you a pendulum swinging left to right. On one side, you are better than everyone else and as it swings to the other side, you are inadequate. The pendulum swings from one side to the other and bumps into those two thoughts. Now it starts to slow down. It's not reaching those extremes anymore. It loses all its momentum. It comes slowly to the center. It rests in the center where the thoughts no longer exist and the only sound you hear is that of you playing as child; who you were before the ego developed. Stay there.

This visual meditation will allow you to face the ego and take control of it.

The Three Personalities

After a year in real estate, I was doing the open house circuit with a buyer on a Sunday afternoon when he turned to me and said, "you're a personality broker." I was stumped by this statement and asked him to explain. He went on to say, "I read an article about how real estate brokers fall into one of three categories. They're either talented with numbers and the market or they have a great personality. The third category is someone who is good at both."

Now, I know what you're thinking and yes, I was somewhat offended by his implication that I am clueless on the market and numbers, but on the bright side, this guy was complimenting the gift I always knew I had; I have a great personality. As for brokers who are good at both... find me a unicorn!

If your talent is numbers and market-speak, you would make more money in commercial real estate, a field that's all about numbers and analysis. It's rarely about emotions and feelings. When someone buys a home, they are making a financial and emotional investment... and the emotional element isn't logical. They need to connect with the property on a level that is almost impossible to articulate. It's something within them (their gut) that chooses the property they will live in. For this reason, a broker with personality tends to understand them better than those who connect with math and the market. This doesn't mean that you have to pack your bags and shuffle off to commercial real estate if you feel as though you don't have this "personality", but it does mean that if you want to work in residential, your personality will serve you. The same applies to those who have a personality and struggle with numbers. Work on the gift you weren't born with.

If you're a numbers broker, I recommend taking an improvisational theatre class. *Improv* isn't just for actors or creative types. I have been in improv classes and many of the students were there following a suggestion from their boss. Improv forces you out of the internal shell and teaches you how to work with others in an uncontrolled environment.

One of the biggest lessons in improv is that you always have to say "yes". When someone asks you to "harpoon a Cadillac!" you must say yes. This allows the story you are co-creating with your teammate to continue. If you say no, you end the game and the story. How does this apply to real estate? Here's an example...

A buyer says they want a larger home but it contradicts their budget and the market analysis. Your gift with numbers wants to tell them, "No, that's not possible." Telling them they don't have the money for the home they want interrupts the story that is unfolding. It stops the dream they have within them for something *you* think is impossible. Saying yes, even if you don't agree, allows you to go back to the drawing board to find the house they want. It might be in another neighborhood or it might be a little smaller but at the end of the day, "yes" is what will get you there.

If you're a personality broker, you would profit more from focusing on the market. Since you already have social skills and understand the client's feelings, it won't be a struggle to connect on a personal level but what's more important, they need to know you can do the work; that you're not just there to have fun. By knowing the market conditions (buyers vs sellers, average price per sq. ft., the current interest rates) they will feel safe when it comes time for you to negotiate the price and the terms. You need to present yourself as a competent broker who can do the job and this doesn't translate if you're gossiping with the client or taking them to happy-hour after showing them homes. I've witnessed super-social brokers lose deals and respect many times. Being social is a money-maker in real estate. No question. But it needs to be kept in check.

When I started real estate, I would chat with my buyers like it was non-stop social hour. We would talk about everything BUT real estate while I was showing homes. I wouldn't consider myself a closer at this stage of my career. This may have been my rookie mistake but I see seasoned brokers doing it all the time and it's partially due to a certain level of insecurity. Many brokers think that their sales skills are minimal so they focus more on getting the client to like them as a person.

Two things can happen when socializing invades the professional relationship: the client doesn't take you seriously as a broker or they might resent you later for having shared too much of their personal information. Think this isn't an issue? Many clients will tell you very intimate social details. Picture it. The seller you're representing tells you about the neighbor who is cheating on his wife. Later, that same neighbor approaches you to sell his home. How will your seller feel knowing that you're going to represent the neighbor after what they told you about him? What if the new client finds out what you know? This may seem like a long-shot but I hear random stories like this all the time. The reason why it's essential to minimize the social banter is due to a code of ethics that isn't part of the contract. So much of what you do needs to be confidential so it's best to keep the personal info, gossip and rumors off the table. When the client goes there, find a sleek way to shut it down and shift the subject matter back to real estate.

LESSON #8

DEVELOPING CONFIDENCE

Wisdom is priceless. It literally is. It cannot be bought. You must have experience in order to obtain wisdom. Wisdom brings confidence. The more you know a subject, the more confidence you have in it. Period. That being the case, the more you know yourself, the more confidence you have. This is what rookies will discover and what seasoned brokers need to take advantage of. My experience working with people in this business has made one thing clear to me: newbies beat themselves up for not knowing everything already and brokers who have been in this business for over fifteen years lack confidence, and for completely illogical reasons.

My confidence in selling homes came from the process of helping people buy them. I think we all can agree that it's essential to work with buyers for a while before we take on a listing and represent a seller. Working with buyers is a process of steps, each of which comes with huge lessons. Here's the process of working with a buyer...

Initial Conversation- You meet someone (could be an office walk-in or in a social setting) and you tell them you are an agent and you represent buyers and sellers. They tell you they want to buy a home. If you haven't done a deal yet or have limited experience, DON'T focus on this. It's irrelevant. Even the most successful brokers on the planet had their first deal and they did it without a clue as to what they were doing.

Now that you know they are looking to buy, the first question to ask before you start pre-qualifying them is... **"How long have you been searching for a home and how has it been going?"**

This question has made me a lot of money. Aside from showing that you care for their story and their experience, you can also get so much information from their answer. Someone could tell you they've been looking for a year (probably not a serious buyer). They could tell you they've been looking for two months and it's been a rat race. This leads you into the next stage of pre-qualifying questions.

Qualify Them- Ask these questions; Have you spoken with an agent yet? What have you seen out there? What is your ideal home and neighborhood? What has your experience been? Have you spoken with a mortgage broker? What's your budget?

I don't recommend pitching your services until you know where the buyer is at. When you have enough information...

Pitch Your Service- People want to be heard and acknowledged for what they want and need. Once the person has answered all the qualifying questions and shared their experience, it will make sense to them why you are pitching your services. Otherwise the buyer will be confused as to why you're trying to help if you don't know what it is they want.

Once you have compiled all the info in your qualifying questions, you can make an offer to represent them. I recommend practicing a pitch that feels authentic to you. My pitch was simple - *"Having an agent represent you makes the buying process so much easier. I would like to help you find a home and advise you through the experience. How do you feel about that?"* At this point, they will either say yes or no. If they say yes, set up an appointment at that moment. Don't say, "I'll send you an email and we'll set something up." Pull your phone out and ask them if they're free on Thursday afternoon (or whatever day is open) for a chat. Give them your card then get their email address and phone number.

Follow Up- Between the initial chat and the appointment, send them an email following up. In this email, ask them to clarify what they are looking for in a home. This is a part of Always Be Closing. Every conversation and email needs to accomplish the next step so don't just follow-up, get more information. For example...

Good Morning, Steve. Great meeting you the other day. I'm sending this email along as a follow-up to our chat and confirming us for our Thursday phone call/meeting at 2:30. I'm going to take a look at your options before we talk. You mentioned that you want a two bedroom home in the Highlands Park area. Feel free to send more information that you feel I should consider while I'm doing the search. Are you considering fixer-uppers? Do you require a finished basement? How much garage space do you prefer? I have a couple people you should talk to as well. First, a mortgage broker (recommend two options with contact info attached to email). I recommend speaking with them before our meeting. It's a short phone call that will get the ball rolling on the financial side of things. Looking forward to your reply and speaking with you more on Thursday!

If you are in a state that requires an attorney to represent the legal aspects, refer two attorneys and attach them to the email as well.

First Appointment- When I was in NYC, the first appointment was typically a Sunday afternoon open house tour. I skipped the formality of sitting at a table to go over details because, for me, it was more effective to get all the important info while looking. At this point, we've already sorted out the financial aspects and what their ideal home is via emails or on the phone. I would send five listings to the buyer and ask him/her to agree to three of them and that's what we would look at that Sunday. I learned more about what the buyer wants while showing them what's out there. However, maybe it's more your client's pace to have a formal table talk. Read your audience and do whatever works for you as long as it's time efficient and gets you to the next step.

Process of Elimination- After looking at a handful of homes, you now have a good idea what your buyer will and will not tolerate. Sometimes you will need to show them listings outside of the area they want to be in. Sometimes you will show them homes that are twenty thousand above their ideal price. During this time, it's all about flexibility on your part. If you try to take them to something they're uncertain about, remind them that nobody is going to die if they look at a home they don't want. This is an educational process for both of you. As long as the listing isn't a complete long-shot, it's not a waste of time. For instance, they've said they refuse to look outside of a specific area because it will lengthen the husband's commute to work. However, there is a home that physically matches their ideal. Once they see it, they will decide a) the extra fifteen minute drive to work ain't so bad or b) the dream home they had in mind isn't all that important and they will take something smaller in the neighborhood they desire. Elimination and learning - that's what's happening when working with a buyer.

What follows is making an offer on the home your buyer wants. Then, negotiations, contracts, inspections, mortgage approval, etc. At this stage, the manager or mentor you have access to will usher you through the process. Here is where your confidence will develop and the next deal, and all those that follow, will become easier.

Confidence is having complete conviction in what you know as well as what you don't. If you don't know the answer to a question, be confident that you don't know the answer. I used to love it when a buyer would ask me a question I didn't have the answer to. I know that sounds odd, but telling a client that you don't have the answer to a specific question is an opportunity to win their trust and shouldn't be taken lightly. Trust is hard to win in this business since many people struggle to trust brokers. Showing them that you'd rather look ignorant than lie to them is a noble path to take and they will be grateful you chose the hard road of not having all the answers over pretending that you do. You can quote me on this, people are better off unhappy with the truth than happy with a lie. Ultimately, the truth comes out. It floats to the surface like a coconut. It leads to angry customers and lawsuits so always tell the truth. Always!

If there is one reason why new brokers stress over lack of experience and seasoned brokers struggle with their confidence, it ultimately comes down to fear of failure. So many choices we make have that word dangling above it. Fear is rarely rational and therefore failure is just a state of mind. Think of it this way, I could "fail" at something and get down about this "failure", but someone could witness the same scenario and not see the failure that I'm focusing on. We make attempts and we get outcomes. That's it. Who decides what failure is? If you didn't get what you wanted, you failed? What if you got something else instead and it turned out to be better than what you were fighting for? Would that still be considered a failure? It's silly, this notion of failure. It does nothing for you. I'm no different than you. I hear the voice of failure and when I do, I acknowledge its existence and then tell it to shut the hell up.

Fear of the FSBO

Where I see a broker's fear of failure the most is when they refuse to make cold calls on a For-Sale-By-Owner. I used to LOVE calling FSBO's. I could pick up a phone right now and call an owner who's trying to sell their property and have a fear-free conversation. The only thing that separates me from a broker who is scared to call a FSBO is perspective.

First of all, what do you have to lose? The listing isn't yours and the worst thing that could happen is they say no, you hang up and get on with your day. Have I been I rejected? Sure. Did I care? No. I can't remember how many times I have been rejected and that's because I really don't care. I don't. It does nothing for me to wallow in a stranger's reaction to me.

Secondly, I looked at owners selling their homes as people who are pretty desperate. On many occasions, after I ask about their experience so far, they respond with a horror story on how its been and I sympathized with them. Genuinely sympathized. This poor person has been trying to sell a home and has no clue what they're doing. If they're choosing to do it *without* a realtor, it's probably for a desperate reason. Instead of using their desperation against them, as many brokers do, I would listen to them for as long as they could talk. At the end of the day, people want to be heard so listening is probably the best thing you can do for a person, especially someone who is selling their own home. I'd even give them free advice. On one occasion I advised the seller on how to sell their home (just a couple of pointers) and after two weeks they called me and allowed me to come over and pitch my services. They gave me the listing and I sold it for them, stress free.

People think selling a home is easy but it's just not. When the cruel reality sinks in, usually after a couple of weeks, they're pretty much ready to hire a realtor in order to end their misery. Keep in mind, if someone is having a miserable experience selling their home and has a concrete reason why they don't want to use a broker, odds are high they have some broker resentment going on and they might be pretty rude when you call them. Knowing this before you dial their number allows you to prepare yourself for ugly comments about realtors. Don't interpret this as a statement about you. They don't know you and if they reject your services to sell their home, it's their choice and it's their loss! Frankly, some people enjoy being miserable and would rather complain about the agony they bring into their lives than hire someone to alleviate that pain. Their choice is not about you; it's about them.

On many occasions, they would ask me flat out *"How much are you charging for the commission?"* I would respond with, *"I'll tell you when we meet but first, let me ask a question: What matters more? What you will pay to have help selling your home or whether you get top dollar from the highest and most qualified bidder?"* Many sellers might respond with *"Why won't you tell me on the phone what you charge?"* I would respond with *"I have a sliding scale based on the work involved so I need to see the property in person. I can go into more detail when we meet."* I would sometimes follow that up with *"I'm curious, what are you afraid of? I'm just going to come over and have a conversation about the market, show you what I can do and if you don't want me to sell your home, don't hire me."* A lot of owners appreciated my candor. I refused to share the commission I charge on the phone. That was a standard I set for myself. If the seller has a problem with it, onto the next one.

Thirdly, remember what I mentioned regarding the difference between failure and outcomes? If you approach a conversation with the thought *"I could fail at this"*, you're setting yourself up. If you approach it with *"This is just a conversation that will lead to an outcome. Anything could happen."* The odds are greater that the call is going to have a better result.

So, here's a challenge; you are going to call a FSBO today. I don't know what your resource is to find this FSBO. Maybe Craigslist, the database from your firm, the MLS... etc. You're going to call this person and simply have a conversation. Don't approach it with a mentality that you are trying to get something out of them. Have a mindset that you are going to *give* them something they need; advice, conversation, consolation...anything. This phone call is about you *GIVING* something to them and, in the world of real estate, that something is always information. Maybe you know something they don't about another listing in the neighborhood? Maybe you can refer a staging company if the house is empty? Be ready to provide them with something they don't have. If you have some information they need, give it to them. This will require doing some digging and getting as much information as possible before the call, which you should do anyway. Having as much knowledge as you can get about the area and the listing will give you all the confidence you need to pick up the phone.

When they answer, simply state your name and what brokerage you're with. They probably get calls from realtors a lot so it's not going to be a surprise you're calling. Tell them you ran into their listing and wanted to know how the selling experience has been so far. They might make small talk and dodge the answer or defend their desire to not sell with a broker. If they just listed it and don't have a story to share, ask them why they have chosen to not have a realtor sell their home. Allow the conversation to flow from here. At this stage you're just trying to establish a social dynamic with them. Be aware of your tone of voice. Being aggressive and talking over them will bring the call to a close fast. Listening is your biggest asset at this moment.

Once you have compiled some helpful information while listening to them, ask if you can meet them in person or come to their next open house to introduce yourself. Say...

"I think I can help you sell your home. I would need to see it and meet you in person to see if we're the right fit. If you're open to it, I'll bring comps from sales in the neighborhood in the past year and discuss your options. I think your experience will be much better with me representing you."

Then hold your breath and see what they have to say. If they reject you immediately, it's your choice if you want to challenge that or not. I have let a couple people go because I could tell by talking to them that they would be hard to work with and I wasn't going to pressure a jerk into hiring me. If they're nice, I would challenge their reason for not meeting with me with the statements I mentioned earlier.

It's a dance, the conversation you have with a possible client. It comes down to your patience and skill of persuasion. If your only reason for not calling a FSBO is because they might say no and you can't handle the rejection, call anyway. No better time to learn how to handle rejection than the present. The more you allow yourself to take the punches of this business, the easier it will be to get over this fear and put yourself in more situations where people will say yes. This isn't going to happen without practice so now's the time.

LESSON #9

PRICING AND PITCHING

If priced correctly, you can sell anything. Whenever a broker rambles on about their listing not selling because there's something wrong with it, that's a good sign they haven't identified the real problem. Either the broker priced it too high or the seller demanded a price well above market and the broker couldn't move them to a realistic number. Either way, the broker is responsible.

I've had many opportunities to take on a listing where the seller suffered delusions of grandeur regarding the value of their property. It takes strength to turn down a seller like this. It takes talent to negotiate this scenario in both the seller and the broker's favor. Once you are comfortable with your pitch for a new listing, you will enjoy doing them and when you enjoy doing them, your odds of winning them is far greater.

Pricing

I can't think of a better way to explain the ideal pitch than to share the story of a listing I had. The pricing conversation was extremely delicate due to the condition of the property. Once this deal was done, it was nominated for Deal of the Year at the Real Estate Board of New York's annual party honoring successful brokers. The category for this award is based on how unique the story of the deal is. After numerous submissions were considered, I was a finalist with two other brokers. You can imagine how crazy these stories truly are in a city so dense with character.

While selling a condo in Brooklyn, I gave an open house tour to an adorable couple who had just begun their search for a new home. They were an eccentric couple to say the least, and we shared fun banter while talking about the current market. When they confessed they needed to sell their loft, I immediately said, "I'll sell it for you." They admired my tenacity and invited me to come by and bring comps. I did more than that, I brought the listing agreement.

When my partnering broker and I arrived at their home, we were pleased to enter a charming, exposed brick hallway leading to an elevator that would take us directly to their apartment. Already there was an appeal to this listing. When the elevator arrived at their floor, the doors opened and we were hit with what had to be the most obnoxious smell I've ever encountered. My eyes burned and I started to cough. The adorable couple, we'll call them Lisa and Lyle, giggled and invited us into the space while explaining the odor. "We have nine cats. They aren't in the best health." As I perused the space, I saw multiple reasons not to take this listing and nine dying cats weren't helping.

Lofts in Tribeca are highly sought after in New York City, and a six floor building with only one apartment per floor is a rare treasure. But that was the sum total of assets. Lisa and Lyle purchased this loft in the 60's. Not a single improvement had been made since and we all know outdated kitchens and bathrooms are a hard sell. Listing the apartment as a "fixer upper" was an understatement. And that, my friends, was only the tip of the iceberg.

Lisa worked at an animal rescue. She was one of the most compassionate people I'd ever met while living in a city that considers compassion highly overrated. She had a soft heart for the animals at her shelter, hence the collection of cats that were on their last legs. Now, if you know what a *healthy* cat can do to stink up an apartment, just imagine nine cats that are dying. In addition to the intense smell from three separate litter boxes, there was the pervasive odor of cat vomit. Lisa admitted that puking events happen roughly three times a day...roughly being the operative word. She spent a lot of time cleaning up after them and warned me that I might have to do a "little cleaning up" myself while showing the apartment on days they weren't around.

While giving me a tour of their antiquated bathrooms and the largest dust covered plant collection in God's kingdom, they went into greater detail with the 'goings on' of the rest of the building. *"There is a lawsuit from the owners against the ground floor apartment. Not only has the owner not paid the monthly condo dues in years, he is also renting his apartment through Airbnb with the tagline Perfect For Orgies,"* stated Lisa. As a resident of New York City, I didn't find this news shocking. What concerned me most, however, was the lack of buyers who want to own a condo in a building that shares legal fees to fight a delinquent owner who uses his apartment as a sex den for tourists.

Mind you, I had shown up with comps in hand and a price for them to consider which, after the tour, became completely invalid. I had hoped to list it for $1.7M. That was no longer an option. The time came to ask the obligatory broker question: "what price do you have in mind?"

"Two million."

Confidence is like a silver tray. It provides a solid presentation of whatever news you deliver, despite the person's expectations. And so I delivered. I asked them how they came up with their number and when they described the neighboring lofty condos that sold for over $1200 per sq. ft., I was more than prepared to go down that road to explain the difference between their home and the others.

They pressed us for the price we had in mind. I can't speak to the experience of brokers outside of NYC but something I observed in my eight years of meeting with sellers, they expect a broker to share their opinion on what the price should be at the pitch for the listing. On many occasions, I would tell the seller I can't price their home until I am in my office and run a comparable report based on the initial meeting. However, in this particular case, I had my partner with me and we both knew the price we would list it for so we didn't waste anytime and stated $1.2M. They rolled their eyes and asked us where we plucked that number from.

It's almost impossible to *not* insult a seller in this scenario so I did the impossible and kindly pointed out the obvious facts (original kitchen/bathrooms, a sex-den with a pending lawsuit, and nine dying cats!). However, this didn't appeal to their sensibilities since they already knew about these things and still believed they would get

71

above market value. They stood firm with the price they had in mind.

A broker in this position has to exhaust kindness and simply say, "Sorry, I'm not the broker for you." And that's exactly what happened. They told us they would speak with other brokers and be in touch. I left with an unsigned listing agreement. Long story short, they met with three other brokers and eventually gave me the listing. They said it came down to my honesty and personality. *Sometimes I think I was the only one crazy enough to actually do it!*

It took more than honesty and personality to sell this apartment. It took strategy and creativity. When buyers called to make an appointment, we warned them that it's a fixer-upper and the odor would be 'intense'. Half the people who heard this declined the appointment so as to not waste their time (and ours). When interested buyers toured the loft and pointed out how outdated it was, we shined a light on the fact it was a loft in Tribeca. When a cat came out of the bedroom and vomited within five inches of a buyer's shoe, I said "It's a sign of good luck when that happens."

Just when we thought things couldn't get worse, Curbed.com posted a lengthy article regarding the sex-den lawsuit on the ground floor complete with pictures of swings made of fur and shag rug pedestals for people to...I have no clue...use your imagination. Selling this loft was going to take an eternity!!! But it didn't, actually.

The listing sold within a month because we had a strategy that we agreed to with the seller. We listed it for $1.4M. If buyers declined appointments after we described the listing on the phone, we would price drop to $1.2M after seven days. At two weeks, we got an offer for $1.150M and the sellers accepted. It was a strategy we knew would work. Lofts in better condition sold for much more, but with the drawbacks of this listing so blatantly obvious, the sellers had no choice but to heed our advice.

As I mentioned before, you can sell anything if it's priced right. If you have a listing with flaws, it's not the flaws that kill the deal. Price it right, it will sell. The art of the deal is in your ability to sell your point of view which involves strategic pricing. Think I'm wrong? I sold an outdated home with nine dying cats in a building with a sex-den with a lawsuit attached and I did it within a month!

Sellers commonly list homes well above their value. Brokers also take listings even when they know the price is too high and they do this for a multitude of reasons. Let's look at two common scenarios...

The owner doesn't really plan on selling, but will do so if someone wants it for a price that's totally unrealistic. I own my home and, if I didn't have better things to do with my time, I would gladly list it way over market to see if some nut wanted to buy it for an obscene amount...and yes I would sell, thank-you-very-much! Sellers like these are a time-suck. You will waste your time with them for a couple months, exhaust your budget and end up empty-handed.

In New York, I would encounter clients like this at least three times a year. I learned the qualifying script to discover the seller's true motives and turned down listings if need be. I'm glad I rejected overpriced listings because when it would eventually hit the market with another broker who didn't know better, it would only take a couple of months for the listing to disappear without a closing; a waste of everyone's time.

A broker is competing with other brokers and wants to get the listing so they recommend an extreme price to the seller. For obvious reasons, this is crooked, not to mention it's a risk that will extend the length of the deal. It takes courage to price a listing right and stand by your talent.

While pitching, I would literally advise the seller of this. I would say, *"Other brokers may come to you and tell you your home can sell for more, but I set this price based on the market, not my personal opinion. I recommend you choose a broker because of their sales skills and not the high price tag."* Sellers appreciated my directness, more often than not, and after they met with a handful of other brokers, they signed with me.

Both of these scenarios involve the listing sitting on the market for over a month with the ideal buyers coming and going. When you eventually drop the price, the best buyers have already seen the listing and have moved on to other properties that were placed in the correct price margin to begin with. Trying to get them back with a price drop is usually fruitless. If a price drop happens to bring in lower price-point buyers, they will question why the listing has been on the market for so long and be suspicious of the price having been lowered. Either way, you can't win.

A skilled broker knows how to present these scenarios to the seller and to do so without alienating or undermining them. It's part of the game of real estate and it's also the best way to garner respect from your clients and colleagues.

If you are absolutely certain what the property should be listed for, stand in that conviction and only negotiate a small margin above it. Any price vastly greater is unethical, will bring you enormous stress and place the seller as the authority on the market, which is a bad way to start. YOU are the authority when it comes to selling homes. That's why people hire brokers. If they knew how to do your job, they would throw their home on Zillow and sell it themselves.

When you have a firm grip on your talents and realize how much you're needed, the effectiveness of your pitches will increase. You are competing with other brokers so, if you want to be taken seriously, you need to stand firm with what you know. That's the broker I would hire to sell my home and that's the broker you would hire to sell yours.

Pitching

After a couple years in the business, my confidence was at its height. I had a couple of brag-worthy deals under my belt, I had more wisdom than the rookies, I could afford an impressive wardrobe...I was a rockstar on the inside and out. Of course, I still got butterflies when I pitched for a listing but if there's one thing I remembered about theatre, if you aren't a little bit nervous before hitting the stage, your heart is just not in it. Don't resist the butterflies or the nervous energy. You can turn that energy into adrenaline, a powerful asset if you can control it. At the end of the day, the pitch is an opportunity to set you apart because odds are, a couple brokers are auditioning for the role. Presenting your unique qualities is absolutely necessary when you're sitting down with a seller.

Seasoned brokers can answer the uncomfortable questions because they've been in the business longer and have seen it all, but you don't have to have years of experience in order to sound professional. When my experience was limited, I started rehearsing in order to sound competent but I continue to rehearse to this day because it allows me to refresh what I already know and feel prepared.

Rehearsing involves considering every statement or question the seller will throw at you and having a response handy. Write a list of everything you think the seller could possibly ask you. How would you handle these questions/ statements...

- The neighbor next door is a hoarder and their property reflects it. How will you handle that when buyers ask about it?

- When can we start marketing? When will the website be made?

- I noticed you have other listings. How do you plan to show mine and the others at the same time during Sunday open houses?

- I have lots of personal pictures hung everywhere and some people told me they clutter up the place and should be stored away, but that's a hassle. Can I please keep them out?

- There is a broker with another firm who specializes in this area. We're thinking of having her over next week to advise us on the right price.

I'm not recommending you memorize possible answers. The process of rehearsing helps to prepare the key words that will be used should those questions pop up. Rehearsal allows you to hear how you'll handle the sticky questions that are always thrown at brokers during a pitch. This practice isn't that different than rehearsing before an interview for a job, which is pretty much what the listing pitch is. Once you internalize the possible responses while rehearsing them, you will be ready to address those subjects. You can do this in front of a mirror, with a friend or even in the shower. Don't be shy or feel foolish about this. Embrace the awkwardness in private so that you don't risk looking awkward in front of the client. Frankly, anything that tests your comfort zone is, in itself, practice for when work and life require more from you than you think you can handle.

Defending your commission is inevitable!!!

Picture this, you're at the dining-room table in the home of a potential client. You've discussed the comps and the price you plan to list their home for. They look over your marketing material, they laugh at your jokes, you are certain the listing is yours and it probably is. Then comes the big question...

"What is the commission you're going to charge?"

This question can elicit cold sweats and nervous energy from both the seller and the realtor because most people get nervous discussing money. That being the case, the more comfortable you are when talking about money, the easier these conversations will be.

Odds are high the seller is going to try to negotiate the commission down to the lowest possible rate so when the realtor says 6%, the seller is ready to ask for 4% in hopes you will find a middle ground. The commission should never be below 5%. At the end of the day, accepting a commission below 5% implies two things; you think you are less than another realtor or you are afraid they will give someone else the listing. It's understandable to have these insecurities but that's exactly what they are... insecurities. So let's do the opposite and gain some security here.

An agent once told me a seller was demanding to only pay a 2% commission because he already had a buyer lined up and he just needed a broker to run the transaction, not the marketing.

We had to brainstorm a reason to ask for a higher commission. I advised him to itemize the commission so the seller will see that the majority of the deal isn't in the marketing, it's in the transaction. There will be a contract to go over with the buyer, there will be an inspection which will change the dynamics of the deal, the buyer might want some last minute changes before the closing happens, etc. Once we discussed the whole scope of what the deal involved, he felt more confident going back to the seller and managed to get a 4% commission on the deal which the agent and the managing broker felt was reasonable.

So many things happen during the length of the deal that have little to do with marketing and open houses, but most sellers don't know that. They think this is a walk in the park for us. They think the broker shows up, takes pictures, makes a cute website and BOOM, property is sold. You have to show them the process of the deal so they will understand what exactly it is they are paying for. Check this scenario out...

Seller-*I don't know...I think 5% will do. I just think that this market is hot and it will sell superfast so 6% seems a bit much. I mean that's a difference of $_____. You see what I'm saying, right?*

You- *Well, first of all, getting a buyer might seem like the easy part but finding the IDEAL buyer out of a stack of offers is an art. I can understand where you're coming from so I think I should offer some clarity with the commission in order for you to see why the standard is 6%. Let's go over the different aspects that are involved.*

Follow that with a description of all the steps in a deal. Once you explain to them the amount of labor that goes into selling their home, they will have a harder time debating your commission. Since you're a practicing agent/broker, you already know the steps in a deal, but in order for you to articulate to the seller why you make 6% on the deal, let's go over the details...

Marketing- This will involve a photographer (which comes out of your budget/commission). You or your firm will be building a webpage. You will write content for the page and create collateral/brochures to issue to buyers.

Open Houses and Showings- Don't be afraid to point out how you are skilled at showing property (verses the other brokers or the seller her/himself). You're the Vanna White of property tours! Don't give away all your secrets, just imply that this is a talent you have. I recommend sharing a story of a listing you sold in the past that was a huge success story.

Negotiating Skills- When you discuss the pricing strategy, you're setting the stage for how the negotiation will go down. Offer clarity to the seller that there are many aspects to a deal that need to be factored in at this stage. The buyer will make requests at this time that are complicated. They will want a certain closing date, maybe a new water heater...etc. Make it understood that you can manage this stage with grace and stability.

Law- Owners can sell their property on a multitude of websites but once the contract comes into play, they are at a loss. Unless they plan to hire an attorney or they are an attorney, the contract is intimidating. You know this domain so take advantage of it by mentioning the contract drafting portion of the deal and how necessary the broker's role is during this stage.

Inspection, Requests and Last Minute Drama- An inspection can lead to requests from the buyer and some of them might be more than the seller should agree to. You can explain how you navigate these scenarios with finesse in the seller's favor. This is another area in which you can tell a story or give an example of a deal that was sailing smoothly and it hit a hurricane right before the closing. These happen a lot and a skilled broker is necessary in handling them. You're not creating fear though, people can see through that and you are better than playing games. You're just stating the real possibilities that they haven't considered and when they realize that they don't want to handle them, because it sounds like a nightmare, the 6% commission starts to make a lot of sense.

Once you've covered all of these, it doesn't hurt to say something cheeky like, "And after closing, I'll set you up with a Wine-Of-The-Month subscription." It's hard for someone to argue your worth when you lay it all out in front of them and then offer them some booze.

If they mention another broker who visited them and offered a substantial cut in the commission, question the validity of that broker. This conversation will lead you to eventually saying, *"In real estate, you definitely get what you pay for and a bargain basement broker will give you a bargain basement experience."*

At the end of the day, don't let your greed keep you from getting the listing. If they stand firm with 5% and you're okay with this, agree to it and move on with the sale. Sellers often want to feel like they're getting a deal so showing some flexibility doesn't hurt. Whenever you negotiate a fee lower than 6%, I recommend a stipulation where they will pay a marketing fee. Therefore, if the deal goes south and never closes, your marketing costs are covered.

Discipline: Pull out a piece of paper and list your attributes. Tap into your confidence and truly boast about yourself. Get extreme with what you think your best qualities are.

My list would include: fast on my feet if the deal goes south, high energy, aggressive negotiator, sense of humor, fashion sense, and so much more.

Now list the things that are *not* your strong suits. My list would include: not detail-oriented, bad at math, lacking patience, and maybe a few more.

This list of attributes will be mentioned in your next pitch. You can either list them one after the other or pepper them into the conversation. Cover at least three things on the list and at some point mention how much you love what you do or how much real estate excites you.

Brokers tend to deflect the spotlight away from themselves and aim it at the firm they work for, but the seller is choosing whether or not to work with you the *person*, not you the representative for _____ firm. They want to know what skills you bring to the table and they also need to feel a personal chemistry and security. It's essential you show them how awesome a person you are. The pitch is literally your moment to present yourself and the perks of communicating with you for a month (or potentially longer), so shine a light on yourself!

As for the list of things that are *not* your attributes, now you know what you must work on. Getting clear with what sets you apart and makes you a rockstar is what gets you the listing. Being equally clear on the things that are not your strong suits is the first step to working on them and shifting your business.

LESSON #10

QUESTION REALITY

They say you can officially call yourself a New Yorker if you have lived there for at least ten years. Personally, I made that timeframe by a hair. Nine years into my residency, I noticed a huge decline in my happiness. My friends were moving out of the city one-by-one due to the high cost of living, marriage and having children. The dynamics of my social life were changing rapidly and I found myself in a rut where I knew I had to make all new friends, which wasn't appealing to me. I was also dating, but that was draining my energy as well. Frankly, aside from my career, I wasn't happy at all. It dawned on me that New York City was a large part of the problem. The subways, the pushing and shoving, the general *toughness* of the city was losing its charm. Just like a dwindling relationship, you know it's over when all the things that you used to appreciate the most become the things you can hardly tolerate.

When it became clear to me that it was time to move on, I was offered a job at another development. It's rare for a broker to move from one development immediately to another so I was excited by this but at the same time,

I was looking for the escape hatch. Since I didn't know where I was going to move to next, I created a strategy that involved taking the job at the new development and stock-piling every cent I made. I wanted to leave NYC with at least $60K in savings and when I did the math on my potential earnings and my cost of living, the numbers lined up so that's what I did.

The new development was a struggle because I missed my old team. It was a long year, but we finished the project in record time. I spent the last five months brainstorming what I would do next and was coming up empty-handed. I started to panic because every option just seemed boring compared to where I was living. The way I saw it, where does someone go after they've lived in one of the most exciting, provocative and highly sought after cities in the world? I had come so far with this career and in a town where the odds of success are slim. Having accomplished so much with so little, it was hard to reconcile leaving. Every option I considered led me to visions of leading a boring life so I started to picture the complete opposite. I pondered how I could capitalize on what I had obtained through all those years of hard work in a merciless city and decided that I should move to another country and sell real estate to rich tourists. It seemed full blown nuts to me...which is why I became obsessed with it and began the hunt for a career that seemed completely unrealistic to me at the time.

Many people live safely within the boundaries of what feels real to them. But let's look at what reality is. First of all, reality is limiting. It's a heavy weighted burden we attach ourselves to in defense of our choices. How many times have you heard statements like...

"I have two kids that take up a lot of my time and energy so I can't travel. That's my *reality*."

"The *reality* is, I don't have time to meditate. Yeah yeah, I'm sure it would help me but sitting quietly for ten minutes isn't possible with my schedule."

"Stefani is applying for jobs at fancy resorts in random countries? Yeah, That's *realistic*! She's a nut!"

That last example is probably what people were saying about me and if *they* weren't saying it, *I* definitely was. Many days I wondered what the hell I was doing pursuing the kind of career thousands of brokers only fantasized about. Who doesn't want to move off to some luxury resort in Italy or the Seychelles, rubbing elbows with successful and unique people, all the while closing deals on yachts?

I decided to think big and apply for jobs that seemed completely unrealistic. I started emailing my resume to random resort developments in exotic locations. Montenegro, Peru, you name it. I was all over the map. This went on for months. I knew in my heart that my experience in development in NYC would garner some intrigue and I was proven right when a top ranking broker responded to one of my many emails. His name was Jim Walberg, a successful broker in the Bay area of San Francisco who I found while perusing the internet for brokers who sold in the Caribbean. He asked me what my hopes were and decided to help me out by connecting me with people in the industry of luxury resorts. Due to the guidance of this kind stranger, I was interviewing with developers who were launching projects all over the world.

I was offered a position at a castle/vineyard in Tuscany but due to the style of the sales team, I declined. Don't get me wrong, living in Italy was enough to accept the limited salary they were offering, but I didn't want to spend my days competing with their staff of six brokers. Another position opened up on the island of Virgin Gorda in the BVI but after researching the developer of the project, his reputation was too scandalous for me to fly there to meet him. I was offered a job selling a development on Manta Beach in Ecuador and accepted it (ignoring the fact I don't speak Spanish). The development lost funding and fell apart within a month of the job offer; before I even had a chance to wrap my head around the fact that this could actually happen.

If there was one thing I discovered while I was pursuing random jobs in random places, it was that it didn't hurt to try. I was only risking time. Time I could have spent pursuing a safer road and moving somewhere pleasant that would allow me to live a comfortable life. But as the months passed without anything to show for it, the search became increasingly unrealistic. That's when I started to wonder...what is reality? If you want to live an unusual, unrealistic life, it will involve viewing your current world as nothing but an illusion. What you are looking at is not necessarily what it "really" is. It's just your interpretation.

I didn't give up on my search because while I was looking, I saw countless developments that had brokers selling them. How were they more qualified than me? How did they get the job? This brings to mind the age-old saying "Somebody's got to do it" and it's true. Somebody does. So why not me? Why not you?

I knew what people were saying about me during that time. I was a single thirty seven year-old deciding to walk away from the security of an established business I created. I heard the occasional veiled complement/warning regarding my courage to take such a bold move, but I shrugged them off. If I hadn't, I would have bought into someone's limited illusion of what I was capable of. I preferred to focus on the crazy possibilities the universe was offering me and to see what amazing opportunities could come my way. I consistently repeated to myself "you have no idea what you're capable of".

People's aversion to risk is due to the mind's preference for safety. The alternative is a scary mystery which will lead someone to potentially leave their job or an insufferable marriage. Even though they're unhappy in these situations, they seem better than the unknown. If you stay in your comfort zone, you won't have to risk anything. You won't have to be surprised by anything and you will live a tolerable life. That is an option...but one of many.

In order to experience change, a little bit of risk is required. You have to risk having your ego bruised if you want to ask someone on a date. You have to risk a major pay-cut to pursue the career you love (like real estate). You have to take risks in order to drop your concept of reality and experience a life that seems unrealistic to you.

"Whether you believe you can or you can't, you're right." -Henry Ford

So can you change your opportunities when you embrace a new perspective? Yes, but in order to shift your perspective, you might have to step outside of what is comfortable to you. Stepping into the unknown isn't a pleasant concept for anyone, so you are not alone. Everyone wants to lean on "reality" in order to defend why they can't level up or take the next big step, but I made the hard choices that lead to enormous discomfort and I not only survived to tell the tale, I did something else that once seemed unrealistic to me...I wrote a book.

And if I can, so can you!

LESSON #11

HOW TO HANDLE A TRANSITION

Once all sixty-two condos were sold in the development I was working on, it was crunch time. I continued to send my resume out to random developers but I wasn't getting the response I'd hoped for. I didn't want to lose all the money I saved paying my expensive rent for another year, so when my lease expired a couple months later, I put all my things in storage and moved to Michigan to live with my mom and dad while I continued the job search.

Once I arrived in Michigan, I didn't feel the emotional stress one would expect after leaving their home and their business of ten years. The last two years had been so exhausting that by the time I left, I grew tired of saying goodbye. I was more than ready to move forward.

Once in Michigan. I settled into my parents' home with complete faith that this would be a three month transition. Once the dream job came to me, I was going to move somewhere exotic and be a rockstar broker. During this time I continued to send my resume out to a long list of prospects, and I watched a lot of Oprah. Five months later, I was still doing the same thing.

Winter is my least favorite time of year. No matter how high the thermostat is set, I'm still cold. The ten degree temperatures and my parents' snow-covered backyard (reminiscent of the set of The Shining) wasn't helping my feelings of being stuck in total isolation. It also didn't help that I was losing hope of getting the job I was desperately searching for. What started out as a lofty ambition, morphed into something that once seemed so possible, and then shriveled up into a fantasy; one that other people get to fulfill. I was in pity-me mode for months and couldn't see my way out of it; stuck in a purgatory between the life I had worked so hard for and another life that was essentially a black hole.

The limiting beliefs started to chime in and the negative wheels started to turn. I felt stuck. If I wasn't moving somewhere exciting, the alternative was going to be a boring struggle I would have to tolerate for years to come. The prospect of having to start from scratch as a broker in a new town somewhere without friends or family gave me anxiety attacks. Why did I leave NYC where I had a job, an apartment in a hot neighborhood and a small handful of friends who loved me? What the hell was I thinking? Questioning reality was coming with a price.

One night I was hanging out with my dad, drinking wine and watching The History Channel yammer on about Sasquatch or UFO's. I don't recall what inspired him to tell the story of the time he took me and my siblings cross-country skiing when we were kids. He told me that when we came to a clearing in the woods, we approached a river that was frozen solid. In the middle of the river, was the head of a deer with its beautiful antlers ascending from the surface of the ice. He described the pickle he was in, having to explain to four children what had happened to this poor animal. The image of the deer came into focus in my mind and continued to haunt me for weeks. I had become this deer.

My dad didn't have an agenda in telling this story, but he didn't have to have one in order for it to have an impact on me. I finally had a symbol that I could connect with. Odds are you have also been the deer. Certainly you've had a transition that didn't go as smoothly as you had hoped. That's why many people fear big change like this. And during said transition, in an attempt to cross from one side to the other, has the tide become so strong you simply couldn't fight anymore? Your legs tired, the water tightened around you and you felt yourself succumbing unwillingly to the cold reality that you can't cross. You give in to the current, feel the blood-flow stop and become conscious of the enormous divide between where you were and where you thought you were going to be.

I once heard a quote: "Something within you must die in order for something else to live." That deer symbolizes the battles we don't always win. The ones where you think you have it all figured out but then the universe or some force of nature decided otherwise. This could involve something as monumental as making a huge life decision or something as fleeting as losing the deal right before the closing. The true test isn't how you master resisting the uncomfortable moments, the true test is in how you accept the moment, accept what is happening. Your spouse tells you they fell in love with someone else. Your mom loses her battle with cancer. You get into a car accident and you are confined to a wheelchair for the rest of your days. We assume these things happen to *other* people until they happen to us. Events happen at work, at home, in the family, to your body. This is life. How do you cope? What are you learning?

Do you obsess on the future or the past? Do you lean more into anger or sadness? Are you aware that these emotions are happening or do you fall into denial because you're one of those people who doesn't *do* the emotion thing. Your connection to those sticky emotions are actually the true mark of what's to come....not the fantasies, hopes and dreams you once had. The only way to see what the future holds is your awareness of how you are handling the present and being open to the lessons that are present.

I wasn't handling the present very well because there I was: mid-winter in Michigan without a job, without a love-life, without a plan. I began to pray to my guardian angels. *"You've been by my side my whole life. You've seen me struggle. It's time to help me."* I'd wait for some divine response: a voice that might come from the ceiling that would tell me what to do. When I lost all patience and decided that the job search was over, I packed my suitcases and moved to Colorado.

I chose Colorado for a multitude of reasons and the number of single men was at the top of that list. The weather is amazing, it's sunny almost all year and even on the coldest day of winter, the sun can convince you it's actually summer. I wanted a healthier lifestyle in which I could hike the foothills on the weekends and hit the slopes in the winter. I also had a handful of friends who had moved there from NYC and others who attended the same college as me and then relocated there. Making the move was easy. I flew to Denver, found an apartment, made a visit to NYC to load my things into a truck and hit the road towards my new life.

It's Exuma, Not Eczema

One afternoon on a beautiful summer's day, just after taking a jog through the park near my apartment, the phone rang. It was a man I had been in touch with seven months prior regarding the development that lost funding in Ecuador. He asked me if I was still on the search for a sales position. When I told him I was, he asked if I would consider selling condos in a luxury resort in the Bahamas. I was thrilled and said yes immediately. He told me the job wouldn't be official until the board of directors met with me. He asked me how quickly I could pack my bags for Exuma. I said "Now!" Five days later I boarded a plane to somewhere I had never heard of.

Telling people I was going to Exuma to interview for a job always elicited the same response..."I'm sorry, where?"

My dad asked, "You're moving to eczema? Isn't that a skin condition?"

Great Exuma is the largest island in a chain of over 300 small islands (cays) whose location is best understood in its proximity to Nassau, its neighboring island and capital. Roughly 7,000 people live on the island (though it felt like a thousand to me) with a minuscule percentage being expats who are either working in the travel industry or hiding/tax evading/running away from somewhere else. Though the Bahamas liberated themselves from the Queen's rule in 1973, you still drive on the left side of the road. The Exuma chain was gaining some serious attention for its swimming pigs.

Yes, pigs. An afternoon visit to a neighboring cay provides visitors with a special greeting from a small posse of pigs living in solitude. When they hear the boat approaching, they appear on the beach and, if coaxed enough, swim out to the boat to retrieve whatever food you offer. This is probably the largest selling point of the Exumas in comparison to the many islands they compete with to get your traveling dollar (like Eleuthera, Abaco, Nassau, Bimini...etc).

I met my contact at the airport and we set out for the resort. When the taxi approached the entryway, iron gates slowly opened to reveal six towering palm trees in the circular drive standing before the guest check-in. After dropping our bags in our villas, we met for a short lunch before taking a tour of the grounds. The resort was comprised of townhouse style villas. Most of them were two floors with outdoor spaces and views of the ocean with a crystal blue shade not unlike a swimming pool. We looked at the restaurant, gym, spa, the beach and checked out some of the town-homes for sale.

Resorts like this are set up as a collection of condominiums. People who own them make occasional visits to the resort and when they aren't there, the condos are rented to guests. The incentive for the owner to buy such a property is knowing that their vacation home is being managed constantly by a trusted staff and the cost of ownership is covered by the guests who stay in the villas. If I got the job, my days would be spent selling the twenty-five condos that were remaining after the other seventy-eight had already sold.

I was surprisingly calm during the interview. There were over ten men present and they fired questions at me regarding my history in real estate. I had complete confidence in my experience and what I could do for this resort, so it wasn't a struggle to remain composed and present my best self. I left the interview not completely certain the job was mine but was content in the fact that I did my best and if the job wasn't mine, then I just wasn't what they were looking for.

The board requested that we put together a price analysis for the listings that were for sale so we met at the bar and ran the numbers. I struck up a conversation with a couple sitting nearby. They lived in Connecticut but spent their earlier years living in NYC. After sharing stories of the town we had in common, I asked them what they thought of the resort. They boasted that their stay was fantastic and planned to return. They told me which villa they were staying in. I took a risk and asked them what they would pay for it. This was partially to help me price it, but also to see if they would buy it. When they told me, *"Oh, at least a million"* I responded with, *"Would you buy it for $825,000? Because that's the price we're considering listing it for."* They looked at each other with a smile, looked at me and said, *"Yes, we'd consider that!"* Long story short, I sold a villa before the job was officially offered to me. That pretty much locked down my position and within a month I put my things back in storage, moved to Exuma and closed my first deal.

The transition that started a year prior was no joke and I'm not the first to tell you that the larger risks have the larger payouts. The thing is, people rarely take gambles with their life choices. Too many fears creep in and before they have a chance to fully envision what their dream life would be, they deconstruct it with all the possible obstacles that could potentially ruin their life. Here's the truth of the matter, those fears are excuses to keep you where you are instead of where you want to be. Any fear that would have kept me in NYC wouldn't parallel the misery of continuing the life I no longer wanted. Though the transition was a long struggle causing me to question everything I believed, it was worth it because it upgraded my standards and improved my life enormously.

LESSON #12

STREAMLINING AND QUALIFYING

When a person calls your office and tells you they want to buy a home, do you start running a search without qualifying them? When someone calls and tells you they want to sell their home, do you immediately run a comp analysis and hurry to their home to pitch for the listing? Learning how to qualify is essentially the act of asking the right question that will determine what is worth your time and what isn't. This is the work-smarter-not-harder concept at play here and that's what I did everyday on that island.

A typical day in my office involved sitting at a desk with the door open allowing the ocean breeze to travel in along with the occasional curious tourist. Most of the people who would visit me were guests in my resort and a small fraction of them were from the neighboring resort that shared our beach.

Traveling to an island like Exuma surprises many people. The assumption is that all the Bahamian islands are all the same, so people occasionally said, *"Wow, there's nothing to do here. I was once on _____ island and there were* countless activities there!" Exuma has the swimming pigs so after you've seen them, you're pretty much spending the rest of your week sitting on a beach or, if you're like many of our guests, asking me to give you a tour of a villa you can't afford.

When a customer enters a typical real estate office, it's a fair assumption that they want to buy or sell their primary home. When people came into my office, odds were high they were two Mai Tai's into their day and had nothing to do that afternoon so they wanted to see some villas even if they had no intention of ever purchasing one. The *real* buyers at my resort could pay all cash and they wanted a tours of what could be their second (or ninth) home, but the majority of people that came through my door could hardly afford the trip they were on. When I started this job, I would give anyone a tour without pre-qualifying but when I realized how much time these lookie-loos were taking out of my day, I had to find a way to decline them. A typical tour can take an hour or more and required a lot of maintenance. On many occasions, a lookie-loo would track sand into a villa or touch accessories and leave smudges in their wake. When a hotel guest checks into the villa later that day and sees sand on the floor or a light that was left on in one of the rooms, they would call management and try to move to another villa or get a free night's stay. This would happen so often that it was affecting the business of the resort so I didn't have much of a choice; I had to intensely qualify people before I gave them a tour. But how do you qualify people who are on vacation? Clearly they didn't speak to a mortgage agent before landing on my island and frankly it wouldn't matter if they did since banks rarely grant loans to condos in resorts. I had to be creative and ask questions about their desire to purchase without offending them. By the time two months on the job had passed, I could size up a real buyer within a matter of minutes. That said, turning down a tour to someone who was bored, drunk and curious wasn't always easy.

I created a time saving technique. When someone came into the office, I would take my time with the conversation. Since they're on vacation, I kept it light by asking them about what events they did that day and how their stay had been thus far. When the topic turned towards asking me about what's for sale, I would show them the availability sheet so they could see what's on the market and the prices of those properties. Once the sheet was in their hand, I would tell them I needed to step out for a second, then I would leave the office. This gave them a sobering moment alone to process the information on the sheet. When I returned, many people would say, "Thanks, no need to give me a tour," and carry on with their day. However, in some cases, people would tell me they couldn't afford to buy but they wanted a tour anyway. At this point I would tell them, *"Absolutely, the next two hours are busy so can you come back at 5:00?"* They would say yes but rarely did anyone return.

You and I know that if somebody wants something, they will make at least a little bit of an effort to make it happen. If they are actually curious about what these homes looked like, they would come back and I'd gladly give them a tour whether I thought they would buy or not.

This is the risk all brokers take. There was always the internal voice advising me to take them on the tour *just in case.* Maybe you have spent plenty of Sundays visiting open houses with someone who isn't ready to buy *just in case,* or you listed a substantially over-priced home with a flaky seller *just in case,* but here's the truth of the matter: you're giving away time and energy for nothing. You have your reasons and that's understandable. Spending this kind of time and energy when you're new to the business is one of many ways to learn, but for those who know this business, the *just in case* reason rarely makes sense. Maybe it's because you're desperate or have a free afternoon but, in actuality, you could be doing something else with your time that would be more profitable. Putting together a mailing, arranging a book club, calling people on your list of prospects, doing a market analysis...etc. I wasn't turning down tours for the tourists because I wanted to play on the internet. Frankly, it would be more fun to give tours than sit in my office alone, but the fact of the matter is, the tours were damaging the property and I couldn't take that risk with someone who wasn't actually a customer. If you're spending tedious hours with a dead-end client out of desperation or boredom, you need to revisit your business plan.

At the end of the day, we all fall prey to spinning our wheels with clients who aren't worth our time. This is more common while working with buyers than sellers since people rarely list their home for sale for fun. When we devote a generous amount of time to someone who we know in our gut isn't the real deal, we're actually doing damage to our self-esteem as brokers because ultimately, the inner voice kicks in and shames you for not converting this person into a real buyer. Whether or not someone is a qualified buyer isn't within your control but choosing to spend your time with them is. Think I'm wrong? Consider the top ranking broker in your office. Do you think they're spending their Sundays at open houses with someone who isn't ready or qualified to buy? That would be a big NO.

Be A Psychic

Intuition is a gift and we all have it. The sonar within you is effective in seeing a conflict coming from a mile away. I'm a little biased because my intuition is very sensitive. I am extremely aware of shifts in energy and behavior and this has helped me tremendously in real estate. For example, I could always smell a deal going south real fast and rescue it before the damage set in. This falls under the Streamlining umbrella. I'll share an example...

In my second year of real estate, after doing only rental deals for the past year, I finally snagged my first buyer. He was the perfect person to represent. He was pre-approved for a loan and had a very clear vision of what he wanted. We found his home within three weeks of looking. He made an offer, it was accepted and we met the broker for a second look before he signed the contract. Afterwards, he left for an appointment and I stayed behind with the listing broker. With a big smile on her face she said...

"You're adorable and you're going to do very well in this business. I can tell you have talent and tenacity, but if you send me a board application with so much as one piece of information missing, I will send it back to you before you can blink an eye."

Clearly this woman had received more than her desired share of bad board packages and was not going to take it anymore.

Side note: Board packages are standard practice in NYC. All homes are condominiums and cooperatives. They have boards of directors who read every detail about the buyer before the buyer can take ownership of the home. If a package is declined for any reason (like missing info or if it's unorganized), they will send it back to the brokers which inevitably pushes the closing date another month or sometimes more.

I admire the statement this woman made, but I was scared of her as well. I didn't want to anger her and screw up our deal but on a positive note, I respected her for saying it. After a couple years in the business and a handful of listings under my belt, I started saying the same thing to brokers who won accepted offers on my listings, especially if they were new to the business or from smaller firms that had shoddy service. I repeated exactly what she had said to me that day. This is a form of streamlining in the sense that you are nipping a common conflict in the bud before it even has a chance to happen. It saved my clients and me many times over. There ain't no shame in telling it like it is in order to preserve your sanity and protect your client, so if you need to warn people or drop a disclaimer, do it.

But let's get back to paradise, shall we?

Effective Listening

Spending a year living somewhere that looked like a postcard 95% of the year was exactly how it sounds, unreal. The days are twice as long when there is little to do. It took awhile for me to make friends since the island is small and people are scattered all over it. Without the Skype calls with friends and family, I don't know how I would have managed the countless evenings I was alone in my villa. Sometimes the island would have power outages and not only could I not call anyone, I would sit in darkness listening to the crashing waves from my balcony alone. It was meditating but isolating. It taught me a valuable lesson, you can be in the most beautiful place on the planet but if you don't have anyone to share it with, it doesn't have much value.

However, the excitement of a deal was the perfect balance. A lot of people posed as buyers because they want attention. I had CEO's talk my ear off about how many homes they own and brag about the size of their boats but all that mattered to me was whether they were a legitimate customer or not. If I wasted so much as one minute with someone who wasn't the real-deal, I was taking a chance. There were many wealthy people who loved the resort so I had to spread a wide net and keep the conversations tight and to the point. I made it clear I was selling homes and when they made it clear they wanted to buy, I gave them all my attention. This would involve a multitude of perks that many visitors wanted to take advantage of; boat & island tours, expensive meals... you name it! I would take a customer on a boat tour out to the middle of nowhere with nothing but crystal blue water as far as the eye could see until we'd reach a sliver of sand as white as flour. We'd anchor the boat near the sandbar and spend an afternoon drinking Kalik Beer and play with starfish. I would treat them to dinners at the resort and spend full days giving them tours of the property and the island.

Since there was a lot of time and money involved, if they weren't a real customer, they were a danger. I had to be extremely sensitive to the words they were saying. If they said things like "just curious", "need a loan" or "we have nothing else to do today and thought it would be fun to spend it with you". Red flags, all of them. I would be held accountable for the money being spent and the time away from the sales office in the rare case a real buyer wanted to see me. Ultimately, this wasn't an issue because I understood the scenario upfront and mitigated the risk by qualifying and streamlining. Once a possible customer passed all my tests, they had my undivided attention until the closing but the only way to know if the deal is real, you must be a good listener...in fact, consider yourself a professional listener. The more attuned you are to the statements buyers and sellers make, the more time and energy you save and can devote to those who are ready.

Streamlining is the skill of saving everyone's time, managing expectations and keeping the deal on its feet before it has the potential to fall apart.

Streamlining Tips

Screen calls. I have recommended this method to brokers and always get a gasp. As if they are committing some terrible act by not answering the phone whenever it rings. If they had an assistant answering the phone for them when they're busy, would they consider themselves evil then?

When I started allowing my calls to go to voicemail, I managed to get more done. To hop-to-it every time someone calls you is cutting into projects you're working on or conversations with people who are standing in front of you (which is rude). An asset to screening a call also allows you to hear what the person wants so you can prepare before you call them back. I had someone tell me in a voicemail that they wanted to sell their home and stated their address. I ran some comps before I called them and sounded like I was a pro in their neighborhood. If a client left an angry voicemail, maybe due to a misunderstanding, I had the chance to do some research to sort it out before I responded with a call back to them to resolve it. I basically treated my voicemail like it was a personal assistant...and a cheap one at that. I never made anyone wait longer than an hour for a response so I still have a clean record for being responsive. Give it a try. Can't hurt.

Add a disclaimer- If there is something about the listing the buyer must know, state it in the listing on the website in full view. After describing the beautiful trough sinks and vaulted ceilings, you can mention that the board doesn't approve dogs that bark a lot (I actually had a board meet with a buyer's dog once. Even though he peed on the board president's carpet, he passed the interview). You can mention that the building isn't accepting investors at this time (if your investor closes and then finds out they can't put a renter in the apartment, you could be sued). You can mention that the home is being sold *As Is* (code-word for fixer-upper and the owner isn't changing *anything* including an old roof or broken boiler).

Qualifying Tips

Ask- Asking someone how serious they are about buying a home or whether they have the financial stability to do so is pretty direct and a lot of people don't appreciate it. I don't mind directness but this isn't the case with most people. There is a delicate balance between getting to the point and respecting ones boundaries but if the client is serious about moving forward, they won't squirm. As I mentioned in a prior chapter, the key question when working with a buyer is "How long have you been looking?" The key question I asked while at the resort was *"How long have you been considering buying a second home?"*. Know what your key questions are and stick with them. They're your money-maker.

Listen- People want to be heard and understood. Once you have asked what their experience has been thus far, listen to the answer in an active way. This is the process of gathering information and it requires focusing on the keywords that are resonating with you. The only way to know more about the client is to listen more and talk less. I'd ask a key question and then keep my mouth shut. If they're talkative, they do all the work for me but if they hold back and have short answers with little information, odds are they're reversing the roles and trying to size me up. At this time, I would put my focus into getting them to trust me, because I am trustworthy. Once they did, they loosened up and the necessary information would come forward. 75% of the people I qualified in NYC were legitimate buyers; only 10% in the Bahamas were. My ability to listen separated the real from the fake and made my job a lot easier.

LESSON #13

JUST ADMIT IT, YOU'RE A SALESPERSON!

Brokers rarely refer to themselves as salespeople. In fact, whenever I remind a broker they work in sales, many of them look confused or offended. All salespeople get lumped into the same category: liars who hustle used cars and bad insurance. For this reason, brokers don't like to admit they're in sales. People are conditioned to think of the world of sales as some slimy profession in which someone is being talked into buying something they don't want. The fact of the matter is, people *need* to buy things and someone needs to help them do it. In real estate especially, people *need* to buy and sell homes; you are there to help them to do so! There, now you can stop feeling so guilty.

I met with a broker recently who told me she's not a salesperson, she's a consultant. Fair enough, but what's really happening here? Sure, she's consulting with people on how to buy or sell a home but ultimately, if she's the listing broker, she is selling a product. Someone is buying something and she's there to do more than just acquisition the deal. You sell your listings and when working with a buyer, you are showing the options for them to purchase. This is sales.

When I was a broker, I also shied away from considering myself a salesperson. A broker, who I considered a mentor, looked me square in the eye and said *"You work in sales and it's your duty to sell!"* He was right. To deny this fact is pointless. Why are we struggling to embrace it?

Our ego is linked to how we define ourselves beyond facts. If you are a salesperson/agent/broker, you are in sales. That's a fact. To say you're not "in sales" in order to hide something involves you putting your ego before your job title.

While representing the seller, I had no problem telling them I was a salesperson because that's exactly what they need. They need someone to *sell* their home, therefore I wore the title proudly. During a pitch the words "I work in sales..." would be peppered into the conversation to help them understand that I was fully aware of what it is that I do for them. I don't talk people into buying things. I sell the best qualities of my listings for my sellers and I help my buyers make a move on a home they want to purchase. One last time, this is sales.

Here's a way to embrace your identity as a salesperson and obtain the buyer's trust. While speaking with buyers, I would literally tell them, "Though I am in sales, it's not my agenda to talk you into a buying a home. You either want it or you don't." I said this because it's the truth. My delivery was comforting and genuine which made them feel I was competent and safe. I assured them that their gut was going to tell them which home was the best option and that I was going to be there to usher them through the process of obtaining what their gut really wanted. This instilled a trust between me and the buyer immediately because, while I was selling them a home, I didn't want them to feel like they were being "sold to". Home buyers are in a vulnerable position and clients bring many different emotions into the process. They need someone who can juggle being a therapist one day and a powerful negotiator the next...so yes, even though you work in sales, you are more than a salesperson.

When you think of it, *everyone* is in sales. Most professions involve pitching an idea to someone or some level of persuasion. The more you shy away from the title of salesperson, the more you risk looking silly because odds are high you will be called out for it at some point. Wear this title with pride and see how it helps your business.

Authenticity

What does it mean to live authentically? To embrace who you are and present yourself to the world without fear? When I was new to real estate, I was scared people would know the truth - that I lacked experience. But when I embraced my position instead of trying to hide it, I realized that it wasn't even an issue for the people who mattered. They weren't focusing on the fact I'd only been a salesperson for less than a year. If, during a pitch, a client did point out the fact I didn't have many listings, I would simply respond, *"This is an advantage to you. I have a big budget and an open schedule. I will dedicate it all to you verses the other brokers who hand the listings to their assistants."*

Ultimately, it's better to know who you are and inhabit your station than to ignore it or pretend to be something you're not. The same applies to your title as a salesperson...that you work in the world of buying and selling...that you are selling a home and therefore, work in sales. Authenticity is an asset and fearing what people think of salespeople is a reflection of you, not the industry of sales.

Integrity is an attractive quality. Those who don't have it acquire a bad reputation in this business while giving this industry a bad reputation as a whole. Those who have integrity struggle to present it to others openly. There's nothing wrong with being bold and saying *I am of my word*, defining it out loud to your client-base. Letting them know you plan to do the heavy lifting, have great attention to detail and care deeply about their happiness is what will set you apart from those who have the same qualities but aren't articulating it.

Insecurity is linked to authenticity. If you're unaware of what's holding you back, this missing ingredient is detaching you from the self. This impedes authenticity. This can affect people who are also a success. I recently spoke with a coach who helps high ranking executives and he observed a common thread between most of them: they felt like they were frauds. They felt that they didn't deserve their success and they have a habit of working overtime to prove they had earned it. When I finally became successful, I too wondered if I had *really* earned it. Had I conned my way into my success? When I reflect back, I think it's clear I earned every dime and credential that followed my name but at the time, I spent a lot of time pinching myself.

Instead of the ABC acronym of Always Be Closing, how about you practice Always Be Conscious? Awareness is the ability to see things at their most basic level and not tinker too much with it. It involves accepting things for what they are (like being a first-year agent or not having the experience you *think* you need) and not letting that fact hold you back. Consciousness of who you are and what you contribute to the world as well as this industry allows you to connect with your self-esteem regardless of how many listings you have or deals you've closed. The alternative is unconsciousness. This is a sad place to be and many people in this industry are unconscious. Focusing on the deal that went south or obsessing on what the broker at the next desk is doing are forms of unconsciousness.

You will have more deals in the future that close or don't close. There will always be brokers who are more or less successful than you. Detaching yourself from the scale that is constantly comparing you to something or someone else is a level of consciousness that will ultimately serve you with something money can't buy, peace of mind. The irony is, peace of mind will improve your business and therefore bring you more money.

LESSON #14

HOW TO PASS A TEST

By the time my contract was coming to a close at the resort, I didn't waste any time finding the next exotic location and had the perfect upgrade project waiting in the wings. Let's backtrack nine months to when I started selling in Exuma.

One slow afternoon (frankly, in the Bahamas, all afternoons were slow) two men booked an appointment with me to give them the lay of the land. This was peculiar since most of my appointments were couples or families looking for a vacation home. These men were investors with a major luxury brand. Their business model was similar to the development I was selling. Their visit to Exuma involved the possible purchase of one of the larger islands as a location for a future development.

Our appointment was to learn more about Exuma and to appease their general curiosity with my resort. The presentation went smoothly and when we were finished, they encouraged me to submit a resumé and contact them when my work with this project was done. Eight months later, I did just that.

After some back and forth emails regarding their next resort in the Dominican Republic, I was flown to Miami for an interview. While they presented the blueprints of their plans to me, I was in absolute awe with what they were building. I'd never seen anything like it. It went beyond a typical resort. It was a master plan that would cover an expansive amount of oceanfront land as well as an elevated portion of the island for a polo field, stables and eco-travel. It's as if they were creating their own town. Prices started at $1.5M for a one bedroom cabana.

The interview continued through lunch and when it was done, they didn't waste any time. They quickly booked my visit to the location. Within three weeks I flew from Denver to the Dominican Republic. I was picked up at the airport and swept off to the site. At this stage of their development, the only finished building was a large villa resting in the middle of one of the most impressive ocean-front golf courses one could lay eyes upon. There was a staff of people on hand to accommodate me with whatever I desired. This place made the resort in Exuma look like child's play.

I had dinner with two gentlemen who were managing the construction. It was a lovely evening. Conversation leaned towards interview banter. I was cool as a cucumber as the tropical breeze funneled through the palm trees and the ocean waves crashed in the background. I was in paradise. The confidence I acquired from years of highs and lows gave me the strength to look at this amazing development of staggering size and know in my heart I would be a success selling it. That is, if I wanted to.

The two days I spent taking a tour of the resort and processing what my lifestyle would be like in this stunning nirvana was tiring. My mind was in full work mode sizing up the gravity of what the job would require and the expectations of those who were hiring me. The night before my flight home, it became clear that I wouldn't have a life there. Moving to this island wouldn't be that different than moving to the moon. Another year of living away from friends and family. I would trade yet another year of planting roots and potentially meeting a life partner for a professional experience in paradise. You know those days when you host an open house during down-season and everyone is on vacation and you're alone for two hours because nobody is looking at homes to buy? That's how I'd feel for a whole year, if not more. I might be sunning on yachts with some amazing people and taking regular flights to and from Miami and New York City, but that's a pretty hollow existence when your gut is reminding you that you don't have a life outside of that. My possessions would remain in storage while I declared myself homeless. My friends would continue to have monumental shifts in their lives and I wouldn't be present for them. There would be births and deaths that I would miss...again.

The whole scenario felt like a test from the universe. I had an amazing and highly profitable opportunity presented to me and saying yes would be as hard as saying no. A couple weeks later, they called me and said, *"We can't tell if you really want the job or not, so it's a no for us. Thank you for your time."* That was the moment when I shifted from uncertain to certain. I was happy that I didn't have to decide. It's as if the universe was listening to my gut and threw me a lifeline. Perhaps I wouldn't have been strong enough to turn it down. I'll never know for sure.

I've heard countless clients and real estate brokers tell me that they don't like their job but they don't know what else there is so they stay on the treadmill-to-nowhere because the alternative is mysterious and difficult. As we get older, mysterious and difficult are bitches. They just are. We have so many parrots on our shoulders giving us their two cents and they feed right into it.

"Squawk, you can't leave a business that took you years to build."

"Squawk, you aren't good at anything else so stay in this job forever."

This voice has enormous power. You can hardly hear it but if you remain in a job you don't like or if you accept a promotion begrudgingly, that parrot is definitely present and it's winning.

Once the job opportunity came and went, I had a bigger decision to make...did I want to leave real estate altogether? I had stockpiled all my money so I had time to decide what my next move was, but when I considered the fact that I had to commit to a place to live and rebuild my business all over again, my gut would chime in and tell me "Don't do it!" That's when I realized that I clearly didn't enjoy real estate anymore because if I did, I'd be okay with starting over. Hell, I would be excited about it. At the end of the day, I would have preferred to take a risk with a new job than slog through a job I didn't enjoy anymore.

I contemplated what my career options were and spent close to a year considering what the best road to take was. The option to be a life coach was, without a doubt, the first time I was completely certain I found my calling. When I was pursuing theatre and real estate, not a day passed where I didn't ask if there was something else out there for me. Once I did research on coaching and the type of people who are best suited for it, I had no doubts this was my destiny.

When people come to a challenge, especially one that reappears in their life, it's natural to feel as though they are being tested. But here's the funny thing, what defines whether you'll pass the test depends on your character and the larger lessons you have to learn. I have discovered that I am impatient and hard on myself. When I am being tested, these aspects come full force. Until I learn the lesson of patience and self-compassion, I will continue to be tested over and over again and when I officially learn the lessons, I will no longer be tested in this way.

"Nothing ever goes away until it teaches us what we need to know."
-Pema Chodron

LESSON #15

SEEK HELP

Therapy has gotten such a bad rap. Why is it considered tragic when someone decides to help themselves using this resource? Many people associate therapy or seeking the help of others (healers, coaches, psychics) as some kind of statement of failure. *"I am seeing someone to help me with my commitment issues"* can be interpreted as *"I fail in relationships and I can't get it together without someone instructing me."* But what is the alternative to seeking help or guidance? The person stays on the same road and continues the same patterns that are not challenging them or helping them to evolve into their better self.

It takes a lot of strength to invest time and money into improving your life and I don't take this choice lightly. At the same time, choosing to embark on healing the pain of the past or establishing a stable future is going to involve discomfort. In order to see ourselves in a way that will create space for change, we have to have a couple gut-checks in the process.

The Subconscious

Do you remember the end of Wizard of Oz when Dorothy is standing before the thunderous and intimidating image of the Great and Powerful Wizard? She's terrified by his hellfire and fury only to discover that he's actually nothing but a simple man behind the curtain, pulling strings and pushing buttons. That, my friends, is the subconscious. He's running the show and he's very much in control. Our limiting beliefs and bullshit behavior are thanks to this man-behind-the-curtain within us. His playbook was written in our childhood and therefore, how you behave as an adult relies heavily on how your childhood played out. How you handle relationships, how you address conflicts at work, whether you can commit to anything or tend to bail when the going gets tough; he's calling the shots and change won't happen until his behavior is recognized. So when my client says...

"Where is the money I'm working so hard for? Seriously, I'm working overtime and have nothing to show for it."

"Women are crazy and dating them is impossible!"

"The other brokers get more listings than me and that will always be the case."

Those are the surface stories that *seem* to be the issue. What's really at play is...

"My business plateaued because I'm tired and need a break. I decline vacations. I stopped doing yoga even

though it was helping my stress level. I get lazy and then I overwork myself."

"I struggle with understanding women's emotions. When they express them, I panic. This might be due to that fact we didn't show affection in my family while I was growing up."

"I fear I'll never level up to where the other brokers are. I was held back in the fifth grade which is proof to me that I'm not as smart as other people."

Just like rattling off the alphabet, large portions of our lives are decided while on autopilot. All our outcomes are essentially a product of learned behavior. We're doing what we taught ourselves to do in our childhood. This is a form of self-preservation and it's consistently limiting the awareness of our potential and dictating how we view our circumstances. Perspective and the subconscious hang out together. Perspective is a large reason why one person is a success at something while another person struggles. This is not the only thing a coach focuses on. Many sessions are playful and don't require journeys into the client's past, but perspective does factor heavily into the work we do.

Who Is A Real Coach?

The "coach" industry suffers from misrepresentation. Many RE brokers who are selling a system-for-success are calling themselves coaches because...well... anyone can call themselves a coach. But if all the "coach" is doing is offering you tips and advice, then they're not coaching you. They're essentially teaching you a system that worked for them. Coaching is only effective one-on-one or in a small group. It's not possible to coach to a massive audience of people who are buying your book, online training system or a speaking presentation. If you've bought into these programs, they were essentially a form of education or training, but if you want a real coach experience, you need to bite the bullet and commit to working with one in a setting where your specific needs are being addressed.

Unlike many "coaches" in this industry, I didn't claim the title until I underwent a formal coach training program. I wanted to be sure my service to the clients that came to me would be solid and based on understanding their specific needs. This involves a larger story than what is happening in the workplace. What hinders all of us, no matter what career we have, is our mindset, something that was originally developed in our youth. A coach is a powerful asset in cracking the code that a person has developed from a history of failure and fear that has permeated their consciousness and created their limited beliefs in their self.

I coach people in many different industries, but my wheelhouse is in working with real estate brokers due to my experience in the business. It is my opinion there isn't one industry where a coach is needed more than in real estate. People who profit the most from having a coach are those who are self-employed. Those who work for a company have the security of the company's support and, since this isn't the case with the self-employed, it is the self-employed who are responsible for creating their own culture and support system. If you want your business to grow and prosper like a large company, you must seek to emulate the same behavior as a large company that has a system in place: one that encourages profitability as well as accountability. Granted, you currently have a manager at your firm but frankly, it's not his or her job to inspire, motivate and hold you accountable in creating your business model. The manager's job is to collect money from the brokers and give you guidance when need be. Your job is to build a successful business that stands on its own two feet. This means that if you ever leave the firm you're currently with, you will have built a marketing profile and a client-base that goes with you. If you depend on your company or the broker-brand that holds your license, your business will struggle should you ever leave that firm. I'm not suggesting that you should leave your brokerage. I'm recommending you build your business as its own entity with the added bonus of having a firm to back you when necessary. The more success you achieve, the more you'll be able to negotiate your commission split which ultimately will define the credibility of your business. It's your duty to get yourself there. Having an unbiased leader (a mentor or coach) in your arsenal will present you with options that your management doesn't offer. This is why coaches are extremely necessary to real estate brokers. I believe this so much I built a business off of it.

In a recent survey, more than 9 out of 10 respondents (agents and brokers) said their business climbed by 10 percent or more during the first year they worked with a coach. More than half said the increase exceeded 25 percent. For a fifth of respondents, business jumped twofold or more, by their reckoning.
-Inman News

People tend to think that their lives are categorical and everything will be awesome once they fix this one problem area. In truth, all the cogs in the watch have to work in harmony for you to know what time it is. Therefore, effective coaching goes beyond what one encounters professionally. Having a coach is also a support system for your personal life. You've heard the term work/life balance; this is where a coach comes into play. Most people excel at one of these things and struggle at the other. Some people focus only on their lifestyle outside of work and wonder why they aren't making more money. Those who are killing it in their professional lives have money and wonder why life outside of the office is a mess. These issues are common regardless of what socioeconomic class you're in. I've seen countless power brokers rake in a lot of money while leaving a couple divorces in their wake and I've seen just as many two-year agents who can't level up their business but have an incredibly fulfilling personal life. In order to have both components of our lives working at their best, one must start with observing the areas in their life in which they struggle as well as where they shine.

For example, I had a client who was exceptional at real estate but couldn't maintain a relationship in his personal life. He bragged that his independent streak was what made him a success at work. He made statements like, *"I never had to rely on anyone to get the job done. I don't even need a partner for my listings."* He worked hard all by himself and is one of the top ranking brokers at his firm. So why can't this man maintain a relationship? Many would say that he puts work before his personal life, but what lies beneath the surface is more complicated than that. Dig deeper and you'll find a boy who was so scared of what others thought of him, he decided it was easier to go it alone in life. He chose to be a success on his own in order to never depend on anyone. Women came and went but ultimately, none of them felt like they were needed. He worked long hours building his business and figured he would one day focus on his personal life and couple-up when the time was right. Here he finds himself in his mid-forties, unhappy with the state of his love-life and feeling lonely. For him, being professionally independent was a bragging right but for his personal life, it was a setback.

This isn't the story for everyone who is single or struggling to maintain a relationship. This is *his* story and once we cracked the code, he had a better understanding of how to treat the women in his life which involved acknowledging that his outlook on being independent was actually validating his fear of depending on someone. Once he made the choice to trust another broker with his business, he partnered some of his listings. This gave him more free time in order to ramp up his dating and he has been in a stable relationship almost a year. Could he have made this discovery while in a power-broker summit or real estate workshop? Not likely.

There are so many questions I ask that lead the client to making discoveries and declaring changes for themselves. One of the biggest questions I can ask a client who is signing on with me is, "What is the biggest setback in your life and what is it costing you to continue living with it?" The answer opens the door for so many shifts to flood in. Your patterns and decisions, whether big or small, impact the quality of your life. This brief life that you have been given – let it not be wasted or squandered personally *or* professionally. My last piece of advice is to know when to ask for help, *real help*, and then be open to receiving it. Live authentically, with purpose and integrity, and just as I have, you will experience truly beautiful and magical things. You will experience an unreal life.

STEFANI**SHOCK**

COACH
CONSULTANT
SPEAKER
TRAINER
WRITER

WWW.STEFSHOCK.COM

ACKNOWLEDGEMENTS

So many people and books influenced what I know and share in my business. Just to name a few...

My Family...

Marianne and John Shock and my siblings John, Jennifer and Diana. All teachers throughout my life.

Friends, Coaches, Guides...

James Dirito, Shayna Ferm, David Hamilton, Joshua Johnson, Kimber Korsgaard, Adiris Salas, Dante Sabatino, Tiffany Bray, Manari Ushigua, Julio Olalla. George Simon Sr.

Notable brokers on my path...

Doug Bowen, Jon Larrance, Jim Walberg, Mark Lynch, Fritz Frigan, Shawn Osher, Sue Simon, Julie Zelman.

...and while on my journey through the unreal choices, thank you to those who believed in me as well as those who didn't. Both were motivating.

BOOKS I HIGHLY RECOMMEND

The War Of Art by Steven Pressfield - Though this book speaks to those who work in the arts and/or creative arenas, it's required reading for anyone who struggles to tap into their create side as well as those who lack momentum.

Start With Why by Simon Sinek - If you ever come to a crossroads or lose your sense of purpose, whether in real estate or elsewhere, this book will offer clarity.

You Are A Badass by Jen Sincero - When I started on my coaching path, a friend recommended this book and a lot of its principles are similar to what I learned in coach school with the added bonus of reminding the reader of their awesome gifts and that they must be shared.

Creativity by Osho - There are so many books by gurus encouraging the spiritual path towards obtaining peace and productivity. This one has all that but will also inspire your creativity...something we all need in our professional and personal lives.

The Alchemist by Paulo Coelho - If you haven't read this yet, it's time. This book is all about intuition and following the magical signs that are present in your life.

The Untethered Soul by Michael A. Singer - This is the quintessential book for anyone who wants to dig deeper into patterns in their life and how they effect our performance personally and professionally.